You Are a Wonder Woman

How to Restore the Wonder and Reveal the Hero in Your Life

BY
ADRIENNE RAPTIS

ISBN: 978-1-915147-88-2 (Paperback)
ISBN: 978-1-915147-89-9 (Hardback)
ISBN: 978-1-915147-90-5 (Ebook)

Book Design by HMDpublishing

“We are perishing for lack of wonder,
not for lack of wonders.”
-G.K. Chesterton

DEDICATED TO

My parents – who made me the Wonder Woman I am

My sister – a Wonder Woman herself

My husband – whose love makes me feel Wonder-full

My children – who awaken Wonder in me daily

My amazing tribe of women – who supported me and helped give me feedback for this book. You know who you are, and you are all Women of Wonder.

CHAPTER *One:*

A WONDER WOMAN IS A HERO

> *"We do not have to become heroes overnight. Just a step at a time, meeting each thing that comes up, discovering we have the strength to stare it down." — Eleanor Roosevelt*

If you picked up this book, there's something deep inside you that knows that you are WONDER Woman. You want to be the hero of your own story. You want to make a difference in the lives of others. You want to go fast, be strong, or maybe you're just picturing yourself in the outfit from the comics or movies. So, what happens? Why don't we always feel like a Wonder Woman? Why did you pick up this book searching for answers? My hypothesis for this book is that we, as women, have largely forgotten our true identities and have lost something we once had as children - the WONDER. This does not mean being a Superwoman in the natural world: it *does not mean having it all*, being the most beautiful, having the most Instagram followers, or checking off a massive to-do list every day.

It's interesting to note that *Superwoman* of the DC comics, is actually Wonder Woman's alternate universe antithesis, who is a self-absorbed and aggressive villain. While I have never been a big comic book reader and this book will only loosely make analogies to the comics and movies, I find this analogy fascinating because it shows us how the ego can turn our actions into vain pursuits. Being a true superhero, however, means a woman who has transformed from living in the natural to the SUPERnatural – someone who has the ability to experience *the wonder of it all*: the ability to look at the world and yourself with fresh eyes and to live in amazement.

You may be familiar with the lyrics from the famous song, "What a Wonderful World" sung by Louis Armstrong.[1] We hear this song, and we all agree that the world is wonderful. There is such beauty in nature and in many of our interactions with one another. So where have we lost the wonder? I think many of us have stopped looking, as we get wrapped up in the mundane, daily tasks on our plate. We see things physically with our eyes, but how much do we really see?

Wonder is defined as: (noun) *a feeling of surprise mingled with admiration caused by something beautiful, unexpected, unfamiliar, or inexplicable.* I think many of us women have lost the element of surprise in our lives. We are often juggling so many activities that we feel we will lose it all if we let even one ball drop. So, instead, we try to control things… but in doing so, we lose the most important things. As humans, we love surprises: a circus, an amusement park, a good comedy routine, or even a horror movie. These all give us the element of surprise. We love being surprised with gifts; it means so much more if we didn't know it was coming. In our everyday lives, however, we attempt to methodically eliminate surprises from our lives. We expect things to go a certain way that they are "supposed" to go - and when they don't, we feel disappointed, disillusioned, and depressed.

So, where do these expectations come from? Many of them are ingrained and culturally conditioned into us. Many others are things we've imposed on ourselves. As women, we have so many more opportunities available to us than any generation before us. We can go to school, vote, own property, and often have a say in when we have children. All these amazing opportunities though have also increased the pressure for achieving greatness and *doing it all.* We can put false expectations on our lives. If you look back at the definition of wonder though, you will see it says, "surprise at the unexpected." With modern technology, however, we often eliminate the surprise in our expectations. During pregnancy (or when we are *expecting*), we can now not only know the gender of our child, but even get 3D images of them in our wombs. Before our children are even born, they are often given names, decorated nurseries, or Pinterest-perfect parties to celebrate their arrival. While I'm not saying any of this is inherently negative, by the time that child arrives we have already put so many expectations of what motherhood or our child "should" be like, that when the baby cries, has a blow-out, or nursing doesn't go as well as what you've imagined, a dissatisfaction can arise in us as we compare our actual lives to those online images we had in our minds.

I often used to joke that I knew the secret of happiness: low expectations. Now, that doesn't mean that we can't set high goals for ourselves or achieve great things. I have my master's degree from Yale, have built a successful business with my husband, have traveled to over 50 countries, have a wonderful family, and have renovated four homes. I was able to do these things because my parents taught me the value of hard work and raised me to have a vibrant spiritual life. I list these accomplishments only to explain that low expectations doesn't mean living a life sitting on the couch watching television and eating Twinkies. Just the opposite: to be a Wonder Woman means setting goals and creating good habits - but also leaving room for the unexpected, wonderful things to come into your life. When we *expect* things to go a certain way or force them into happening, we lose the magic, joy, and wonder that life wants to show us.

If you are with a significant other, how likely would they be to stay with you if you forced them to love you? Expectations can grow as a relationship grows, but a real relationship is all about freedom for individuals to grow because of your proximity to one another. I think life responds to us in a similar way. When we try to control the outcomes and expect life to go in a specific manner, we too quickly close the unexpected doors that are available to us.

Sometimes a door may look on the outside like a negative outcome. As I write this, we are in the middle of the coronavirus pandemic. Many of us think that life was not supposed to happen this way. We can all relate to this time no matter when you read this book because you can think back and remember how you felt when this happened. Were you frustrated that life was not happening the way you expected it to? But where did these expectations come from? No one in your life ever told you that a pandemic wouldn't happen to you: quite the opposite. There have been many books and movies over your lifetime that have warned you of this possibility. We never expect sickness, being laid off from a job, death of a loved one, or being cheated or lied to. But if we look at the probability of those things happening based on statistics, there is actually a high likelihood of many of these occurrences during our lives. Of course, we don't want to go seeking the negative things in life or we are sure to find them. We just shouldn't be completely thrown off balance when the bad comes along. After all, Wonder Woman is a hero. She trains for a world where bad things happen. If hard things didn't happen in the story of Wonder Woman or any story at all, the hero would never emerge, and it would be a very boring story indeed. So, here's the question: how can you train yourself to be the hero in your own story and turn the unexpected negative things in your life into the times when you shine? How can you flip the script?

To paraphrase Mariah Carey's song, "*Hero*,"[2] you need to look into your heart and not be afraid of who or what you see there. If you reach deep inside and uncover the things you've been hiding, the hero inside you will cast away your fears and help you discover love and pursue the dreams you've been holding on to or the dreams you have let go of. While this may sound nice, and if you take a moment to play the song, it may inspire you, how do we, as women, take *practical* steps to create a *practice* of looking into our hearts and reaching deep inside? If you notice those two italicized words in the previous sentence, they are very much related. They both come from the same word, *practisen*, which means "to follow or employ" a course of action. In this book, we will follow some practical advice given to us by our Creator to help you transform your thinking to understand the WONDER-full life you have been given and the mission you were created to accomplish.

Reflection Questions for Journaling or Group Discussion

- Do you currently feel like the heroine of your own life? Why or why not?

____

____

____

- What negative things are you currently facing or have faced in the past? Are they defining you or can you re-define them to see them in a new light of how they are helping you emerge as your own hero?

____

____

____

- Where do your current expectations come from? Are they helping or hindering you?

____

____

____

CHAPTER *Two:*

A WONDER WOMAN HAS A MISSION

"Everyone has his own specific vocation or mission in life; everyone must carry out a concrete assignment that demands fulfillment. Therein he cannot be replaced, nor can his life be repeated, thus, everyone's task is unique as his specific opportunity to implement it."
- Viktor E. Frankl

Your mission, should you choose to accept it:" these are the classic lines from the *Mission Impossible* series. All of us would probably say we want adventure, right? Would you say you also want to be part of a mission in life - to have some greater purpose? Although audible message telling us our mission would be nice, life doesn't really work that way. Or does it? Humor me for a minute. What if we were given our mission when we chose this adventure of life as humans on this planet? What if we are really citizens of another Heavenly realm - amazing and wonderful spirits of light who chose to come to this planet to experience an interesting journey of being in material form? What if the memory of all this, or the metaphorical "tape," had to self-destruct for us to come have this human experience? I've observed in my own life and through the writings of others, that children are innately more connected to the spiritual world. They don't have to be told twice that they are Wonder Woman or Superman. They believe it. Their imaginations are incredible superpowers. They can create whole worlds, and magic is real to them. When you look at the word "imagine," you can break it down into "I-magi-in." The word Magi as it appears in the Christmas story, were the wise men from the East who came to worship Christ as a young child. Magi is related to the word magic.

Do you believe in magic? Kids do. As adults we may not believe in magic in the same way, but we must admit we still appreciate it. We go to magic shows and are thrilled with the illusions. Someone who performs magic is really someone skilled in knowing something you don't. Our brains perceive things in ways most of us do not understand. We think we see what is true, but brain researchers show us that our brains are often not able to perceive or receive all the signals accurately. Magicians use this to their advantage to create illusions.

Well, what if this whole world is a grand illusion created so we could experience the game of life? What if you are already a Wonder Woman who has just forgotten. In the movie *The Incredibles,*[3] the superhero family was forced to live as mere mortals because people were afraid of their power. Their children even thought they were weird because of the powers they possessed. But nothing was wrong with them except that they had untapped power and were frustrated by that.

I have a secret for you, in case you don't know already: you are a child of God. Say those words out loud. I AM A CHILD OF GOD. Sit with that for a moment. How did that make you feel? Did something inside you resonate? Did you feel a chill? If not, repeat those words until you feel it. The word resonate means to produce or to be filled with a deep, full, reverberating sound. In physics, it's the reinforcement of a sound by reflection from a surface or by the synchronous vibration of a neighboring object. Now, please don't give up on this thought just because I used the word physics. In simpler terms, it's the tendency of a system to vibrate with increasing amplitudes at some frequencies of excitation. God is trying to get your attention. He's trying to awaken you to the fact that you are His child.

In Luke 15, Jesus tells a story about a son who asked his father for his inheritance to be given to him while the father was still alive. When he received the money, he went off to a distant country and "squandered his wealth on wild living." To this end, he was forced to find a job feeding pigs and was so hungry he wanted to even eat the pig slop. Verses 17-24 states the following:

When he came to his senses, he said, 'How many of my father's hired servants have food to spare, and here I am starving to death! I will set out and go back to my father and say to him: Father, I have sinned against heaven and against you. I am no longer worthy to be called your son; make me like one of your hired servants.' So he got up and went to his father. But while he was still a long way off, his father saw him and was filled with compassion for him; he ran to his son, threw his arms around him and kissed him. The son said to him, 'Father, I have sinned against heaven and against you. I am no longer worthy to be called your son.' But the father said to his servants, 'Quick! Bring the best robe and put it on him.

Put a ring on his finger and sandals on his feet. Bring the fattened calf and kill it. Let's have a feast and celebrate. For this son of mine was dead and is alive again; he was lost and is found.' So they began to celebrate.

No matter what you have done in the past, the Father longs to open his arms to you and welcome you back as His child. If you have been running, its time to stop and remember who you are. There is a better life awaiting you if only you would accept His invitation and the mission He has given to you.

We have been sent into this world to play an adventure game. Imagine for a moment that this whole universe is an awesome school for the children of God. We are sent here to learn, to grow, to figure out how to get along with others, and, figuratively, to not put glue in our mouths. This illusion we live in is so realistic though that we've forgotten why we were sent here in the first place. We got trapped in the lower vibration of the material world until we started to think that the stuff around us was all that mattered… and we even call it that – matter.

After God made the universe, He made us in his image, with the ability to think and create things. The man-made world is a manifestation of our collective thoughts. If you look around you right now, wherever you are, all the things you see: the clothes you are wearing, the seat you are sitting on, the building you are in, the food you just ate - all these things are in existence because someone somewhere first had the idea to make it. It started with a thought and then that thought became a reality. But the figurative school bell is starting to awaken us from this reality, calling and exciting us to live at a higher vibration. God wants us to awaken us from the illusion so that we can really immerse ourselves in this playground he has given us.

An example of resonance is a playground swing. The person pushing the swing has to match the timing of the swing. Imagine God is the parent pushing the swing and you are the child. If you sit tight and hold on, you can have a fulfilling moment and an excited experience. God will push you higher and higher. You will be in sync and your joy will soar. But what if you, as the child, started jiggling in your seat, swaying side to side – wanting to go in a different way? You would lose that synchronicity. How often do we do this though and in our daily lives get off track? God isn't always asking for our movement. He just wants us to sit and be in harmony with him and give us joy because He loves us.

What if, when we are born on this planet, we had to give up our knowledge that we are spirit beings because it would be too much for us to handle? The infinite powers of the universe are available to us when we connect back to God. When we are born, however, like the genie in the lamp, they must be put into "itty bitty living space." The genie is the genius that is living inside you that is just waiting to come out of the lamp. The lamp is now being rubbed. Like the *Incredibles* family had to step out and not be afraid of their powers, the resonance of this vibration is starting to wake you up.

Have you ever been sitting in the same position too long and your foot fell asleep? Of course, you have. As I am writing these words, I too have noticed my foot was asleep. When you start to notice this, you don't let it stay in that state. You get up and start moving. By your movement, it awakens other parts of you. As humans on this planet, we are all children of God. Every single one of us. Yes – even that person you can't stand right now. We are all here in this adventure, or school of life. Some have been awake to this knowledge for a while. Some are awakening and some are asleep. My goal for this book is to get us moving and awaken the parts of us that are asleep.

What excites you? What passion gives you energy? Like organizations have a mission statement, you too can create a mission statement for your life. I wrote out my personal mission statement in college. When I needed help making a decision, I could determine if that choice was in line with the mission, and it helped guide me in many different situations.

When Christ came to this earth, he not only showed us how to live, but he also left us with a larger mission. His last words are recorded as what is called "the Great Commission:" Matthew 28: 18-20 says, *"Then Jesus came to them and said, 'All authority in heaven and on earth has been given to me. Therefore, go and make disciples of all nations, baptizing them in the name of the Father and of the Son and of the Holy Spirit, and teaching them to obey everything I have commanded you. And surely, I am with you always, to the very end of the age."* There are many books written about one's purpose in life, and of course we all have unique gifts and talents, but when it comes down to the nitty gritty of our purpose and mission, this is it: our *co-mission* together on this planet. This doesn't mean that you have to necessarily go to another country to be a "mission-ary." You are a missionary wherever you are. The gospel is the good news of love, and if you have received that love, you simply need to share that love with everyone you meet. While that might sound all touchy-feely and gushy inside, learning how to truly love everyone often requires sacrifice and humility. This is the example Jesus gave. He literally gave up his life to show his love for us and break the bonds of sin and death that held us captive to this world. His resurrection showed us how, we too, can gain eternal life by giving up the things that ensnare us.

Reflection Questions for Journaling or Group Discussion

- Do you feel like a child of God? What does that mean to you and how does knowing that change how you view your life in this world? If you have never prayed or asked God to come into your life and adopt you as His child, please contact me at wonderwomanhealthcoaching.com and I would love to pray with you.

  ____

  ____

  ____

- Have you ever written out a mission statement for your life? If so, remind yourself of what your mission is or take some time to ponder what your mission statement would be.

  ____

  ____

  ____

- Do you feel as though life is like a game? If it were, how would you approach your trials or just your everyday life differently?

  ____

  ____

  ____

CHAPTER Three:

A WONDER WOMAN GIVES UP TO GAIN

We must be willing to let go of the life we have planned, so as to have the life that is waiting for us. - E. M. Forster

Spoiler Alert: If you haven't seen the Disney movie, *UP,*[4] I'm about to give away a key scene, so you may want to skim over this. The movie is from 2009, so it's not exactly new and I'm guessing many of you have had the opportunity to see it if you wanted to. If you haven't seen it, there's an elderly widower named Carl who is a retired balloon salesman. He and his wife always wanted to go to South America, but never got the chance. When his wife dies and he is being told he needs to go into a nursing home, he gets the idea to blow up thousands of helium balloons and fly the house to South America. At one point in the film, he needs to get the house off the ground again to help a young boy who accidentally stowed away in the house. To get things moving, he starts throwing out all the furniture to make the house lighter. He gets rid of those things he once cared about so that he could be the hero for this little boy.

When you picture a hero, what is the first thing that comes to mind? Is it a person in a cape? Is it a sports star or your favorite actor or actress? Is it a firefighter, teacher, doctor, or nurse, or the person who delivers your groceries? The Covid-19 pandemic widened a lot of people's definitions of what a hero is. But the thing all heroes have in common is that they give up something. During the pandemic, we acknowledged heroes as those who gave up their own personal safety to help others. Sports heroes give up a normal life for one of intense practice and training. Our screen heroes give up, for a time, who they are so that they can portray a new and interesting persona.

In Matthew 16, Jesus says to his disciples, *"Whoever wants to be my disciple must deny themselves and take up their cross and follow me. For whoever wants to save their life will lose it, but whoever loses their life for me will find it. What good will it be for someone to gain the whole world, yet forfeit their soul? Or what can anyone give in exchange for their soul?"* What Christ is saying here is not a threat of death, but an invitation to an incredible life. We may not physically die on a cross, but we can put to death our egos and our small lives in order to gain the abundant and eternal life He offers to us.

To play a game well, you need to give up what you're holding on to. You must pass the ball, show your cards, give up some monopoly money to buy the hotel… I think you get the picture. Have you ever tried to play fetch with a puppy who just wouldn't drop the ball? The game could be fun, except the puppy won't let go of the ball so that you can throw it again. I think we as women can sometimes be like that puppy. We hold on to things so tightly that we can't enjoy the game. It may be material things we're holding on to or it may be something more abstract. How many things are you trying to juggle? In 2020, women, for the first time ever in the US, held a greater percentage of American jobs, excluding farm workers and self-employed individuals. While we may exclaim this as a triumph for women, we all also must admit that we are now trying to carry a burden that we are sometimes feeling crushed by and juggling more and more.

The thing about juggling is that you can hold onto something, but it must be very loose. Hold it. Let it go. Hold it. Let it go. The better a juggler can let go, the more things he or she can juggle. A master juggler can receive more and more items even as they juggle the items they have. If I, as a non-juggler, were to try to receive something thrown at me, I might accidentally drop everything I have held tightly in my hands while attempting to receive that one thing – and may end up dropping that item as well. If you had your grandmother's antique teacup and had to choose between passing it to a juggler or just any person off the street, I'm guessing you'd trust the master juggler. They have practiced juggling fragile things and are less likely to drop it. We too, are more likely to be entrusted with special treasures if we can daily practice the art of letting go.

One of the characteristics we all picture when we think of a superhero is the ability to fly. Do you think that Wonder Woman could get off the ground if she had any baggage with her? Of course not. The image is laughable. But think about when you fly. How much do you need? This may hit a lot of us hard because we, as women, are notorious for bringing too much baggage compared to our male counterparts. It may come down to the simple idea that we feel that we are not enough. If you need to bring a lot of makeup on your journey, is it because you feel like you are not beautiful just as you are? If you need a lot of clothes, do you feel you won't be loved or appreciated if you don't portray a certain image? These are tough questions to ask of ourselves. But if you want to really be free enough to fly, you should look at your baggage.

I recently challenged myself to truly fly as a "Free Spirit" on a Spirit flight to visit my sister after she had a baby. Spirit flights are cheap (mine was $49 roundtrip), but then they charge you for even carry-on luggage and where you sit on the plane etc. Since I was flying alone, I didn't have to sit anywhere in particular or bring all the baggage I would normally have when flying with children. I decided to see if I could roll all my clothes into one handbag and fly without any luggage. Imagine the freedom I felt strolling in – not even having to roll a bag! As a matter of disclosure, I did mail gifts to her before I left and I also rent most of my clothes, so I had my shipment mailed to her house, but it felt great to travel with just the bare necessities.

Do you remember that song from the movie, *The Jungle Book*, called *The Bare Necessities*[5]? You can find the lyrics online, but to paraphrase, we need to keep an eye out for the things that are the most important or essential. Too often we're running around chasing after so many things. We're stressed, trying to get more and more and then working to hold on to it all. We need to realize that the necessities of life will come to us if we just learn to let go. It reminds me of something that was spoken by Jesus many years ago. Matthew 6:25-34 says:

"Therefore, I tell you, do not worry about your life, what you will eat or drink; or about your body, what you will wear. Is not life more than food, and the body more than clothes? Look at the birds of the air; they do not sow or reap or store away in barns, and yet your heavenly Father feeds them. Are you not much more valuable than they? Can any one of you by worrying add a single hour to your life? "And why do you worry

about clothes? See how the flowers of the field grow. They do not labor or spin. Yet I tell you that not even Solomon in all his splendor was dressed like one of these. If that is how God clothes the grass of the field, which is here today and tomorrow is thrown into the fire, will he not much more clothe you - you of little faith? So do not worry, saying, 'What shall we eat?' or 'What shall we drink?' or 'What shall we wear?' For the pagans run after all these things, and your heavenly Father knows that you need them. But seek first his kingdom and his righteousness, and all these things will be given to you as well. Therefore, do not worry about tomorrow, for tomorrow will worry about itself.

We hear these words, and they sound so nice, but how do we do this in practice? We have mortgages or rent, and we have kids that we worry about constantly. As mothers, we're professional worriers. But God wants to guide us from *worriers* into *warriors*. Part of letting go is simply learning to delegate and allowing others to hold the ball for you. Delegating means training someone else to take the reins and be okay with the fact that things may not be done exactly perfectly as you would have done them.

The word delegate comes from Latin *delegatus* 'sent on a commission' - so as you learn to delegate, you bring people into the mission with you. While you must release control to be able to delegate, you are also stepping back in humility and acknowledging the things you do well and the things that you don't. There are many things over the years that I have learned to delegate. There are people that are trained to do certain things much better and faster than I could. When I learned this, the business that we own started to take off. No longer was I pulling out my hair trying to do everything. I could now focus on the things that only I could juggle and give the rest to people who I trusted to juggle even better than I could.

With modern technology, we can now let others go grocery shopping for us or do many other time-consuming tasks. While many people first started getting groceries delivered during the pandemic, I have been doing this for a long time and could probably write a book on this topic as well. While you may spend a little more on the service or the tip, I save so much by shopping the best deals at each store, easily seeing the sale items at each store, and only buying what is necessary. How many times have you been at a store and spent way more than you intended because you were tempted by this or that? It's not good for your wallet or your waistline. If they don't have delivery services in your area, one good thing that has come out of the pandemic, is all the drive-up services that are now available. This is a godsend for mothers with young children. I don't know how many times I wished I could have had someone just bring something out to my car in the past when my kids fell asleep. If I want something at a store with drive-up service, I can now just order it from my computer or phone, and they can bring it right out to me. This saves time and the frustration of your kids (or you) wanting things that are not needed. With the phone in hand, you can look through your pantry or fridge and see what you really need. You can explore new recipes and find ingredients which would have otherwise taken you forever to find in the actual store. While it may initially take more time to get used to the delivery service or drive-up apps, they will be a game changer if you take the time.

If you truly enjoy going to the grocery store or other stores, then, by all means, keep doing it. Each of us is unique in our likes, dislikes, passions, and pains. There is no one-formula-fits-all, and what may work for me may not work for you. These are simply suggestions for you to look at your list of all the things on your to-do list and to find ways to give yourself some extra time and freedom. The goal is to create space in your life to be free and live a life of wonder. In the next chapter, we are going to explore a secret weapon to help us eliminate the extra baggage from our lives and fly in the way we were intended. In the next chapter, I'm going to let you in on an important secret to letting go and going fast.

Reflection Questions for Journaling or Group Discussion

- What are you holding on to that you could give up to God?

____

____

____

- Create a list of all the things you are trying to juggle. Circle the top things you dislike or that take up a lot of time. Then think of a creative way that you can hand that ball off to someone else and delegate it to others or meditate on whether it's something that even "needs" to be done in the first place.

____

____

____

- What are your main worries or concerns? What if you decided to not worry about them? Would it change anything?

____

____

____

CHAPTER Four:

A WONDER WOMAN GOES FAST

Fasting is the greatest remedy-- the physician within. – Paracelsus

A wonder woman doesn't just fly. She goes fast! She has people to help and superhero things to do. So how do we do these same things? The secret is hidden in plain sight. Go fast. If you are not familiar with fasting, it is the giving up of something - usually food or drink, but it can be other things as well. It has been taught since the times of Hippocrates in the 5th century BC as a therapy for prevention of various illnesses. Paracelsus wrote that fasting is the greatest remedy. Almost every tradition in the world has extolled its ability to bring both physical and spiritual renewal.

Our western society is so focused on self-indulgence that we have lost the art of self-control… and we wonder why we feel depressed, aren't motivated, or are sick. Your body is an incredible machine, capable of wonderful things and of healing itself. When we see Olympians or other sports heroes, the things they can do with their physical bodies is astounding. Those individuals know the value of their bodies and treat it with care. They don't give their "machines" junkie fuel but take care to give it the best they can. The Bible calls our bodies the temple of God (1 Corinthians 3:16). A temple is defined as a building devoted to the worship, or regarded as the dwelling place, of God.

If you viewed your body in this way, would you put junk in it? So often, our bodies are sick because they're trying to tell us that we've allowed toxins to invade. Or perhaps the army of our bodies, our immune system, has not been given enough good ammunition to fight off invaders, like a virus or bacteria. The art of fasting allows us to detoxify our bodies and clean our temples so that we can more clearly hear from God and be the wonder women we are.

I think a lot of us view fasting as something too difficult for us. Giving up all food is indeed a major challenge, but like I said with the baggage, don't get overwhelmed. A little something is better than nothing. Start small. Pick out one thing that you want to fast from. You could start with just a month, a week, a day, or even just one meal. Wherever you are, start there. You can't start from anywhere else but from where you are anyway.

A Wonder Woman is free. You may not think you're a slave, but are there things that you find it hard to live without? Obviously, I'm not talking about water, air, or basic nutrients. What I'm referring to is our addictions. We often think of addictions as being only to things like drugs, alcohol, or cigarettes. If you are addicted to those things, these are difficult addictions to overcome because of their strong chemical components in our brains. If you need to, there are many professional resources and groups that can help. Addictions are like a ball and chain around our legs. We may have a desire to fly, but we physically can't.

Your body knows what it wants to be free from. It will tell you through the way you feel. For years, I knew coffee and creamers were not good for me, but I ignored it because I thought it wasn't a big deal. Coffee may be totally fine for you, but for me, personally, I discovered this one small thing caused a downward spiral in how I was eating and feeling. If I had coffee, I wanted just a little biscotti or cookie to dip in it…or maybe two. The coffee made me jittery, so then I would need to eat more. I think I may also have a dairy sensitivity, so adding milk wasn't the best for me either and I also used way too much sugar. I was a slave to it though because I couldn't live without it. Then, one year, I decided to give it up for lent. I had never practiced lent before, but I felt something in my spirit tell me to do this. Of course, it was hard at first, but I started feeling so much better in so many ways. Then, another month I gave up alcohol. I didn't consider myself a heavy drinker, but when I started tracking my food intake, I realized how often and how many empty calories I was consuming. I've struggled with my weight my entire life. I've had gym memberships, but the workouts never made that big of a difference. By fasting this one thing, the pounds just started to come off. The main reason, I believe, is because fasting is a spiritual practice, while dieting is just depriving without getting anything in return. When you fast, you are not just giving up something; you're being filled with something simultaneously. You're giving up the natural to gain the supernatural.

Fasting allows you to look more clearly within and analyze the reasons that you go to whatever it is you feel you need. If you feel like you need caffeine for energy, fasting allows you to break free from that and get your energy from the true source of all energy. If you need alcohol when you feel stressed or are in social situations, fasting helps us address the roots of our stress and anxiety. I've realized that I turn to sugary foods when I feel life is sour and salty foods when I'm bored and what I really need is some spice in my life. Fasting from those things allows us to discover triggers and deal with the root of the cravings. Unless you deal with the weed at the root, it will always come back. That is why you always gain weight back after dieting. Sometimes it takes multiple rounds of fasting to really address the root too. You may think you've taken care of something, but if even a little piece of the root exists, the weed can return.

I periodically do the Daniel fast, which is a 10 day fast of not *how much* you eat but of *what* you eat. It is really what we should be eating all the time: eating mostly fruits, vegetables, and whole grains and avoiding meat, dairy, stimulants, and processed foods. The name of this fast comes from *The Daniel Plan*[6] book, written by Pastor Rick Warren, and inspired by the book of Daniel, where he proposed to the King that he and a few other of the King's advisors eat only vegetables for 10 days while the others stay on their standard diet. Daniel 1: 15 says, "At the end of the 10 days they looked healthier and better nourished than any of the young men who ate the Royal food. So, the guard took away their choice food and the wine they were to drink and gave them vegetables instead. To these four young men God gave knowledge and understanding of all kinds of literature and learning. And Daniel could understand dreams of all kinds." It also goes on to say, "In every matter of wisdom and understanding about which the King questioned them, he found them 10 times better than all the magicians and enchanters in his whole kingdom."

Do you see the difference that this made to their mental capabilities? When I did the Daniel fast for the first time, the thing I was most surprised at was the mental clarity I felt. The benefits of fasting are as easy as ABC: A- Alignment, B- Breakthrough, and C- Clarity. If you can picture your body as a planet, I want you to see the blood vessels that feed your brain as rivers and streams. Do you want clear, fast flowing streams or murky, polluted waters? Our SAD (standard American diet) eating habits have led both our physical world and our inner world to be polluted.

According to the American Heart Association, the maximum amount of sugar a woman should have per day is 25 grams. If you've ever looked at the back of that "healthy" yogurt you're feeding your kids, there can be 25 grams just in that alone. The average person typically eats around 70 grams of sugar per day. Sugar is highly addictive, just like any drug.

When I first did the fast, I thought I had addressed the roots of my own sugar addictions, but they came back with a vengeance when Christmas rolled around. Have you ever noticed how religious holidays have been hijacked by the candy industry? I hadn't made this connection until this fast. Our culture pushes us to believe that every holiday and every celebration should be marked with a huge hit of sugar. I'll leave my rant on this for another book, but it is truly a candy conspiracy that we need to get out from under. My mind had felt so free and able to receive insights when I was eating pure things, and then when I started eating junk food again, it literally felt polluted.

In Mark Hyman's book, *The Ultramind Solution*,[7] he explains the biological pathways that lead to either a clear or toxic mind. I highly recommend this book if you want to discover how to eat to heal your body and your mind. Another great recommendation is *Change Your Brain, Change Your Life* by Dr. Daniel Amen.[8] By the way, these two doctors co-wrote *The Daniel Plan* with Rick Warren. Warren approached them because he knew that he and his congregation needed to get healthier and that the way we are living in our modern world is not the way God intended for us. The book is also very wholistic in its approach and focuses on five key essentials of faith, food, fitness, focus, and friends – because all of these things are integral for an abundant life of freedom.

These two doctors have been revolutionary in their practices because they focus on nutrition to heal and prevent disease. If the Hippocratic Oath is literally translated it says "I will apply dietetic and lifestyle measures to help the sick to the best of my ability and judgment. I will protect them from harm and injustice." Far too many doctors today prescribe medicine that is merely a temporary patch for problems that need to be addressed at a much deeper level. They are barely given any training in nutrition in our medical schools, but instead are pushed from day one from the pharmaceutical industry to prescribe certain drugs, which can often lead to negative side effects.

If I were to give you a prescription today, I would recommend a whole food, mostly plant-based diet to anyone I meet. While I eat meat from time to time, I try to make sure it is high quality and that the animals who gave their lives for my nutrition were given a decent and humane life and death. As a disclaimer, although I studied nutrition in my undergraduate years, have my master's degree in public health, and am a certified health coach with the Institute for Integrative Nutrition, I am not a doctor. Before you begin any fast or changing diet, consult a doctor who you feel has your best interest in mind. I recommend someone who has studied functional medicine or takes a holistic view on health. Find someone who will truly guide you and take time to listen. Medicine and prescription drugs certainly have their place in our lives, especially when our health deteriorates beyond a certain point or if there are certain injuries etc. I encourage you though, to take a proactive, preventative approach to your health. If you don't have your health you can't show up for life in the same way. Your health is your wealth.

After shifting my eating habits, I was able to lose the weight naturally and easily. It's not about looking a particular way or fitting into some mold that the magazines or media portray. It's simply about becoming the best version of you that you can be. It's about living confidently and being capable of showing up to follow your dreams. Forget the fad diets or the quick schemes. This is about transformation. This is about the start of an amazing journey of discovery and growth. This is about being able to have the strength and stamina to go fast. But first there's something you'll have to do along the way.

Reflection Questions for Journaling or Group Discussion

- What are you a slave to? Do you have certain things that you feel like you should fast from in order to break free?

  ____

  ____

  ____

- Do you view your body as the temple of the Holy Spirit? If you did, how would it change things for you?

  ____

  ____

  ____

- If you have weight you want to lose, brain-fog you want to get rid of, or any other health issues you want to resolve, how could changing the way you eat improve your life and make you feel Wonder-full?

  ____

  ____

  ____

CHAPTER *Five:*

A WONDER WOMAN TAKES IT SLOW

"The great benefit of slowing down is reclaiming the time and tranquility to make meaningful connections–with people, with culture, with work, with nature, with our own bodies and minds"
- Carl Honoré, In Praise of Slowness: Challenging the Cult of Speed

Take it slow? Isn't that contradictory to going fast? There's always some mystery in the irony. This book was birthed in the midst of the coronavirus quarantine, where we were all forced to go slow. This is not my natural inclination. As far as my personality type goes, I'm an enneagram seven. If you are not familiar with enneagram, I encourage you to read about it and discover your own number. It's an awesome tool for understanding your personality because it goes deep into your fundamental root desires. Enneagram sevens are characterized by always being on the go. We hate being bored and have a gluttony for life. My friends call me the "Duchess of Muchness" if that tells you anything. I'm always doing too much. I'm the "Hostess with the Mostess" and have already done thousands of things on my bucket list. I've met numerous presidents and world leaders, skydived, hot air ballooned in Turkey, traveled by myself to Bali and whitewater rafted, worked in shantytown orphanages in Africa and Central America, and have met hundreds of famous authors. As the owner of a rare bookstore, you can imagine that I like to read. For my 40th birthday, I had 40 goals and just one of them was to read 40 books. Yes, I'm that "muchness." But just before this pandemic happened, I had written in my journal that I felt like a hamster spinning on its wheel – always going, but not getting anywhere. It took a pandemic to help me to slow down - and let me tell you, it has been so good for me! I know that so many people struggled at this time, but I've also heard from many people how they thrived by learning to shift their thinking and behavior.

I've always wanted to write a book, but it wasn't until I had slowed down enough that I could really put down the words that I felt God was trying to convey to me. It was also on day two of a fast that I started writing this. Although I had fasted certain foods before, a two day fast gave me the mental clarity that I needed. When I was fasting, I slowed my body down. I didn't do regular workouts. I rested. There's an amazing thing that happens when our bodies rest: they heal themselves.

There's a reason that the observance of the Sabbath rest is one of only 10 commandments. I think this is probably the one we break most often. We see the obvious moral problems with murder or adultery, but we let ourselves off the hook for not observing the Sabbath. I'll raise my hand as the first to admit this. God wants to heal us and help us remember who we are. If you break down the word, *remember* into re-member, you can see it involves us coming back together as members of the body of Christ. We are one body with many parts. When we rest and come together for the Sabbath, we heal our egos that make us believe that we are separate.

Corrie ten Boom once said, "If the devil cannot make us bad, he will make us busy." It seems like our world is busier and more hurried than ever. We "normally" live at such a fast pace. Although we have more gadgets to make life easier, we've just added things to our lives to increase our busyness. If you are a mom with kids and have them in extracurricular activities, you understand the rush of taking them here and shuttling them there. I talk with so many women who feel like they run a taxi service for a living. We feel like we all must keep up with what our neighbors are doing. Although social media and sites like Pinterest and Instagram can be a positive place to share with one another, we get trapped in the "despair of compare," thinking that we are not doing enough compared to someone else's picture-perfect life. So, we pile more things on the To-Do List. We push our kids to do the activities so that they will get into the best schools. If we have careers, we want to be the best in that too, all while maintaining the picture-perfect home. Never in the history of the world have women experienced so many (albeit false) pressures to do and have it all.

We've got to end the craziness. It is not good for us and it's not good for our children. In Esther Wojcicki's book, *How to Raise Successful People*[9] she talks about how kids need to have space to grow. As the mother of three successful women (one is the founder and CEO of the company *23 and Me*, one is the CEO of YouTube, and one is a professor at UCSF), she has a lot of wisdom to share if you want to pick up this book. Another good read is *How to Raise an Adult*[10] by Julie Lythcott-Haims. The premise of both books is that parents are currently doing too much for their kids, and it's detrimental to their development. Parents have been caught writing their kids' college essays, doing their kids' college homework, and even trying to come to job interviews with them. The madness has to stop, for their sake and your own.

So let me cross half the things off your To-Do List: stop doing so much for your kids. You'll be happier, and therefore, a better mom to them, and they will develop some grit and be more self-reliant. Stop making separate meals for them because they don't like something. You need to eat healthy and so do they. If you want to get healthy, you've got to minimize those unhealthy foods you're buying for your kids and secretly eating. If they want a treat, they can earn it by helping with tasks around the house. Having kids help around the home not only helps you, but it trains them in the long run to be organized, disciplined, and confident that they can one day live on their own - which is the general goal (unless you want them living with you until they're 30).

Wow. I hope you feel lighter just thinking about all that extra time you have now. OK, let's see how we can get some more time for you. Look at your to-do list. How does it make you feel? Is the word overwhelmed? That's how I often felt when I looked at all the things I "had" to do. The thing about being overwhelmed, is it's like a wave crashing on your head. You can get disoriented and, hence, not able to do the very things you wanted to do. It activates your stress response, and so you turn to tv, social media scrolling, food, or whatever it is you like to distract yourself with.

So, get rid of your to-do list. Seriously - or at least hide them somewhere. I suggest you make a "to be" list instead. Think of the characteristics of the person you want to be. Is it stressed? Probably not. Is it joyful? I'm guessing you'd say yes. If the end goal of why we are doing all the things we're doing is ultimately to find happiness, why not just skip all the to-do's and just be happy? Easier said than done, right, but why is this so hard? Why do we feel this pressure to be constantly doing? In the Bible, there's the story of Mary and her sister Martha in the gospel of Luke chapter 10. Mary sits listening at Christ's feet while Martha is busy in the kitchen cooking and cleaning. Martha complains to Jesus that Mary is not helping her, but Christ tells us that Mary has chosen a better way. You see, if Martha really knew and understood the power of God, she wouldn't worry about preparing a meal for the one who multiplied 5 loaves of bread and two fish into a banquet that could feed 5000 people. If we understood the power of God, we wouldn't be chasing after so many things that don't ultimately satisfy us.

If we don't slow down and just be, we'll miss out on all the WONDER that God wants to show us. I recently felt convicted of this and felt that I needed to take a week to fast from my phone. We're so connected to technology in today's world, we literally can't escape from it. Whereas, just 20 years ago most of us didn't even have a phone, now it seems we can't live without it. Just like a drug, our brains literally light up like a hit from a drug every time we hear a ding or vibration. *Did someone like my post? Who's texting me now? I need to respond to that email urgently.* Personally, I love my phone mostly for the photo and video apps. I'm a serious photo-aholic. I have an online album with 10,000 photos each of my kids. Yes… I really am that muchness. In many ways, I love photography because it allows me to slow down and see things in a new way. I bend down to observe a flower or get an interesting shot of a bird.

But just like any good thing, you can take it to the extreme, and I obviously was taking it to the extreme. Instead of using photography in the way I just described, I was using it *instead* of seeing. I would view an entire sunrise through my camera instead of viewing the sunrise itself. My phone was always by my side - and I knew it was bad when my mother started calling it my third appendage. It was becoming an idol in my life, and I felt God was telling me that I needed to give it up in order to gain. Anyway, I decided to try to go without it for a week. As a disclaimer, I do have a watch phone as well, so I could take emergency calls and such, but it was still a challenge to break free from my phone. Let me tell you, ladies, the amazing things that happened just by taking away this one thing.

On the very first day, I went on my usual sunrise run. I am blessed to live by the ocean and take a run most mornings at sunrise and photograph the sunrise on my phone. Of course, it was the most amazing sunrise, and I was missing my camera, but I have a few friends who take professional photos, so for this day, I rested in the fact that I would see their photos and just enjoyed the sunrise. I didn't have my usual music as well, but it was nice to be in the stillness of the waves. And then the most WONDER-full thing happened. I saw a dolphin! I've never seen a dolphin on any of my runs, so I credit the fact that I was paying more attention. I pointed out the dolphin to another woman who was on the beach, and she suggested that we try to swim with it. While the dolphin didn't come up to us or anything, we had a beautiful swim, and I made a connection with another wonder woman who shares my interest for the environment and cleaning the beaches. Her husband had died this past year and I was able to share in her grief. Even amid the coronavirus, we hugged there on the beach - this stranger that I had never met. On another day on my beach run, I felt the Lord was giving me a song. A friend of mine had sent me a card with the words, "Be Still and Know that I am God," on the cover. It was also the topic of the day in the Bible study I was currently doing. Now, I am not a songwriter in the least, but these are the words I was blessed with as I took the time to be still. You can read it as a poem.

Chorus: { Be still and know that I am God
Be still and know that you're my child } 2x

You are my own. You are never alone.
And I am here with you.
I am your guide. I am right by your side
Amid the rising tide.

I'm your strength and your shield.
If you only would yield to the mystery of my love

Though I've always been near, you're too busy to hear
Of my unending love
Quiet your soul. I am still in control.
And I will speak to you.

It's a still, small voice so that you have a choice
To love me in return
I'll bring peace to your mind that you never will find
Anywhere but me

When the rain pours down, my grace will abound
When you cry out to me
My blessings you will see

I hope you like this song even if you don't have the tune, but whether you do or don't is not the point. Ladies, I wrote a song! That's the amazing thing about being quiet enough to be inspired. Life is teaming with creativity. We just need to catch a little bit of it. Earlier in the year, my mother-in-law had given me a card I wrote to my husband when we were dating. It had been in his old bedroom, and she found it as she was going through some things. In it, I had written some of my dreams. One of those was to play the guitar well and write my own songs. I had completely forgotten about a dream I once had. I never played the guitar well, but I had been learning more when I wrote this. I had saved up for a beautiful red Ovation guitar and loved playing. But in the years of busyness, that guitar got pushed to the side and stayed in its case. My daughter recently asked me to get it out, as she was interested in playing it. I took it out of its case only to find it had been damaged during our recent renovation. There were even broken pieces in the chamber that I had to remove. It still plays, but it was out of tune.

The analogy here is that in all our busyness, we ourselves have gotten out of tune. We have gotten out of the practice of being in harmony. If you remember from Chapter 2, we talked about resonance. Another classic example of resonance is playing a stringed instrument, like a guitar. Resonance works in a guitar when the strings transfer their sound into the body of the guitar and set up an internal resonance in the air chamber made by the body and cause the back plate and face plate to vibrate. These vibrations cause the air to compress and rarify making the compression waves in the air that our ear interprets as sound.[11]

We need to allow ourselves to get in tune with God so that He can create a masterful song out of our lives. By keeping our bodies, or our chambers, clear of the toxins, it's like when I had to remove those broken parts out of the chamber because it was making the whole instrument sound strange. When I cleared those pieces out and tuned it, the air inside compressed and rarefied. I love that! As a seller of rare books, I know the value of something that is rare. We all love rare things. We value them because of their scarcity. Professional musicians have perfected their craft, and people pay a lot to attend their concerts. When you hear something truly beautiful, you stop what you are doing and listen. That is the power of music, and that is the power of what God wants to do in your life.

Reflection Questions for Journaling or Group Discussion

- What is your view of the Sabbath? Do you regularly take time for rest and reflection? Why or why not?

____

____

____

- When was the last time that you allowed yourself to be creative just for creativity's sake?

____

____

____

- What are some practical things you can do to remove distractions and slow down? Write down a list of things you want *to be* instead of all the things you have *to do*.

____

____

____

CHAPTER Six:

A WONDER WOMAN IS A MASTER OF TIME

"An inch of time is an inch of gold, but you can't buy that inch of time with an inch of gold. – Chinese Proverb

When I was in high school, I wrote this little poem about time:

Time passes, unnoticed
By no fault of our own
Seconds, minutes, hours, days,
How the years have flown

Count the minutes missed
Of nothing really done
Wasted time that can't come back
Unfinished things that were begun

We rarely get the chance
To do something so great
As to be remembered in this life
When we are passed of late

So if you get that chance
Don't wait one second more
Use the talents given
And you'll see great things in store

I rediscovered this poem this past year. I don't know how old you are, but if you think back to high school, there have probably been many minutes that have flown by unnoticed. So, my question to you is, what are you valuing? Where are you spending your time?

If you are serious about slowing down and finding time for the important job of becoming the wonder woman you were meant to be, you'll have to start setting priorities. The word priority comes from the Latin term *a priori*, meaning something that is known ahead of time. Setting priorities of who you want *to be* instead of things you need *to do* shifts the focus and creates time where it was previously lacking. Why do some of us seem to have more time than others? So many of us can never seem to "find the time" for things. The question is… where did it go? We are all given five hundred twenty-five thousand six hundred minutes in a year, as you may know from the famous song, *Seasons of Love*[12] from the Broadway musical, *Rent.* If you are not familiar with the song, you can look up the lyrics, but the idea behind the song is that we need to measure our time, our seasons, and our life by the amount we love and are loved.

Are we measuring our time in love or do we measure ourselves by all the things that we do or money that we make? Most people are familiar with the phrase, "time is money." Most of us think that means that to earn money, one must act and therefore use one's time. But this is only one aspect of money. Money should be a tool - not an end goal. A tool is something that we use to make life easier and free us from time. A car is a tool that saves us time getting from one place to another. A dishwasher saves time in doing dishes, and a washing machine saves time in doing laundry. All these modern conveniences have saved us more time than ever before in the history of the world. In the past and even in many parts of the world still today, women, in particular, have had the job of getting water from wells or streams. This one task can even take an hour or more. In the Western world, we take it for granted that we have clean water piped into our homes exactly in the location that we want it. We should all feel like royalty every day with all the amenities we have. Even the queens of history did not have the luxuries that we do. So, why don't we have all the time in the world if we are saving so much time? It has to do with the way we are *spending* both our time and our money.

We need to focus our attention on *using our money to get more time* and managing both to the best of our ability. There's a phrase, "time poverty" that keeps coming up in things that I am reading. At the end of the 20th century, the term, "Money-rich, time-poor" was an expression which arose in Britain to describe groups of people who, while having a high disposable income through well-paid employment, had relatively little leisure time as a result.

This is an unfortunate phenomenon, as it is totally preventable. It is a blessing in disguise that we were forced to slow down during the coronavirus pandemic. While we may not have been making as much money and it was a struggle for many to even put food on the table, I've heard and seen so many people spending more time as a family, taking bike rides, playing games, and in general "having more time." We still had the exact same number of minutes in our day and year, so why did it seem like we had more time? It is because we were spending it on things that mattered, which created the feeling of having more of it. We were measuring this season in love.

So, let's look at how we are prioritizing our time and money, so that we can continue to create that feeling of being time-rich instead of time-poor. One thing I noticed about myself in the past year is how stingy I would be with my money when it came to getting help. I don't know if it's my New England work ethic, but I never used to get help cleaning even though we had a nearly 8,000 square foot house. (FYI, this was prior to having kids). Anyway, I could easily spend the same amount I would have spent on a house cleaner on a run to Target or elsewhere to fill my home with more things that I then had to clean. We don't want to just spend our money; we want to invest it. We want to make a return on it. Most of us think about investing money for a financial return, but few of us think about investing in a *time return.* If you have $100, which would be the best use of it? 1) hiring someone to help you clean (thus saving about 5 hours of cleaning yourself), 2) buying a new outfit or 3) buying food for your family. Wait a second. Whoa. This is a hard question. You thought I was going to give you a no-brainer, right? Wrong. You must use your brain. You must think ahead of time, what is your priority? It all depends on your personal budget and the goals that you set. If you have a job interview, perhaps a new outfit is the best use of your money. The word invest comes from the Latin *investire*, meaning "to clothe in, cover, surround" - so it might be a good investment for both your time and money to be able to earn more if you got that job, so that perhaps you can afford to have a house cleaner etc. Putting food on your table is obviously a priority over a perfectly clean house if this is the only $100 you have, but if you have already allocated money to food, would it be wise to spend more than necessary on food? If you're spending too much on food then perhaps you are eating too much, and thus need to also purchase that gym membership to work it off, which results in a time deficit. I know this is all simple enough to think about, but so often many of us are not considering these things when prioritizing our budgets.

Now, even Wonder Woman herself does not have the ability to manipulate or travel in time. People have dreamt of time travel for ages. From studies in physics, we do know that time and space are related and connected in some way. Scientists even refer to it now as spacetime. So, while we are in this space, we can't really stop time. I remember this show when I was growing up called *Out of this World*, where the main character was a girl who was actually half alien and had the power to stop time by just putting her fingers together. Anyone remember this show? Anyway, although she was not really supposed to use these powers, she often felt tempted to do it. While she often had good intentions, she sometimes got herself into trouble.

You see, space and time are the tools that we can use to be present in this world. The present is our gift, which is why it is called this. We often miss out on this, but the past and future don't exist for real. They are constructs in our mind. There is nothing else but the present. Try to get to the past… you can't do it. Try to get to the future, you can't do that either because by the time you get there, it will be the present. The biggest way I have found to stop time is to experience things deeply. Can you think of a time in your life or a day that just seemed to last forever? I know when I was young, the summer just went on and on. A day at camp felt like a lifetime. When you travel, it seems like you've been away so long because you have experienced so much. You come back and realize that all the people that you left didn't experience time in the same way you did. Or have you ever done an intense workout? The other day my daughter was trying to lead me in 2-minute workouts - two minutes of jumping jacks, two minutes of push-ups etc. Once we got to plank, believe me, that two minutes seemed like the longest two minutes. But it was the same 120 seconds that everyone else experiences.

Or, on the opposite side of the spectrum, there are moments when time seems to speed up, usually when we're having fun. During these experiences, we're spending time more freely and are usually happier. When it comes down to it, the search for happiness is why we do most of the things that we do, so having fun is not a bad thing… but I do have to point out this caveat that we have to be careful with this, as our culture focuses so much on pleasure. We are constantly being entertained.

If you look at the history of the decline of civilizations, you'll see a constant theme - they began to have too much of a focus on being amused. Amusement is defined as "anything which pleasantly diverts the attention" (from duty, work, etc.) The word was originally depreciative, or causing something to diminish in value, and derived from French military action in the late 15th century: "to divert the attention, beguile, delude," from the Old French *amuser* "fool, tease, hoax, entrap; make fun of," literally "cause to muse" (as a distraction). It also originates from the Greek term *amousos*, which meant "without Muses," hence "uneducated." I love the visual from the story of *Pinocchio*, where he finds himself smoking, drinking, and playing billiards on Pleasure Island, which ends up being a trap. Once the boys have enough time "having fun," they would turn into donkeys after they made "jackasses" of themselves.

I'm concerned that our western culture is not only beginning to decline, but we may already be on that slippery slope. Our children don't want to work hard because they like playing video games or watching tv. It's more fun and much easier. They don't see the need to have goals because they have been given so much. I am the first to admit that I got caught up in this. I realized that my children were becoming entitled to having fun when my oldest complained one day that she didn't have fun that day. It brought me to a halt. There are children working in sweatshops and begging for a piece of bread and here is my child complaining that she didn't have fun! We want to give our children good experiences, but there is a pressure in our social media to create all these over-the-top experiences for them. Seriously, the extravagant birthday parties have to stop. What are we teaching them?

We need to figure out our priorities because our *motives* create the *motivation* in our lives and our *emotions* about things creates the *motion*. When we think about what we really, truly want, it will change our behavior. If we really want to become wonder women, we need to prioritize creating space and time for that wonder, both for us and for our families. We don't just want a little wonder in our lives. We want to be wonder-full. Create room in your calendar and prioritize wonder.

Instead of just writing down all the things I wanted to get done on a particular day, I have started putting things on my calendar like "hugs for my family," which happens at 7:30 am. My husband and daughter need physical touch from me to feel that they are loved, whereas I feel loved when people do things for me - so I needed a reminder that my act of service to them was to make sure that they are receiving that from me daily.

As a side note, if you are not familiar with the *5 Love Languages*[13] by Gary Chapman, I recommend this book as well. The five love languages are: Words of Affirmation, Acts of Service, Receiving Gifts, Quality Time, and Physical Touch. We all have one or two that are most prominent, so it can be very helpful to determine yours and that of your loved ones so that you can love them in a way that they feel loved.

Going back to the calendar, I've started writing things like, "be present with my family" as one of my top 3 priorities each day. It doesn't matter what I do if I'm not actively experiencing the present. As we learn to prioritize, we need to look at the things we spend our time on, which means we need wonder-full vision. We'll explore this in the following chapter.

Reflection Questions for Journaling or Group Discussion

- What would you say are your top 5 priorities? Does your calendar reflect these priorities?

___

___

___

- Take a look at your budget or your credit card statement. What are you spending your money on? Is it reflective of what you want to value?

___

___

___

- Name one way you could spend your money differently to create more time for yourself.

___

___

___

CHAPTER *Seven*:

A WONDER WOMAN HAS SUPER VISION

It's not what you look at that matters, it's what you see.
– Henry David Thoreau

What is your vision? It's your ability to see what is going on around you - or a little more scientifically, it's your brain's ability to perceive light and the way it bounces off the matter around us. We know that some of us have better vision than others because some of us have to wear glasses or contacts. Perhaps we see things too close or too far. This can happen in a metaphorical sense as well. Sometimes we need to do a metaphorical assessment of our vision to know whether or not we are seeing things accurately. Just like going to the eye doctor helps us know if we need glasses, if you don't regularly look at your inner spirit's vision, you may get into an accident. Ask yourself what lens you are looking through. We all see through different lenses. Every human on this planet sees the world through their own eyes and their own perspective. We have to question how accurate this lens is though? When our son was 4, he didn't like wearing goggles when he swam underwater because he said he can see underwater. The chlorine had been hurting his eyes sometimes though, and I wanted him to wear goggles occasionally. Anyone who has worn goggles underwater knows the difference it makes over just opening your eyes without them. You can see, but the vision is blurry. When we finally got him a pair of goggles he liked, he couldn't believe the difference.

I believe our dreams (both nightly and our daydreams) give us insight into this (it's literally in-sight, in case you didn't catch that). Many people have gotten into the practice of making vision boards, which are a great way for you to physically see with your eyes the dreams that you want to manifest in your future. In 2019, I made my first vision board as part of a "Busy Women in Business" book club that I was in. Like many people, I had the thought of having 20/20 vision for 2020. Little did we know then how much vision we would need. What a year it was! The way that I put my vision board together though actually really helped me to see this year so clearly and thrive at this time because I believe I figured out my priorities. As I was thinking about my vision board, I kept coming back to the words of a hymn that I used to sing in church called *Be Thou My Vision*. Here are they lyrics:[14]

1. *Be Thou my Vision, O Lord of my heart; Naught be all else to me, save that Thou art. Thou my best Thought, by day or by night, Waking or sleeping, Thy presence my light.*
2. *Be Thou my Wisdom, and Thou my true Word; I ever with Thee and Thou with me, Lord; Thou my great Father, and I Thy true son; Thou in me dwelling, and I with Thee one.*

3. *Be Thou my battle Shield, Sword for the fight; Be Thou my Dignity, Thou my Delight; Thou my soul's Shelter, Thou my high Tower: Raise Thou me heav'nward, O Pow'r of my pow'r.*
4. *Riches I heed not, nor man's empty praise, Thou mine Inheritance, now and always: Thou and Thou only, be first in my heart, High King of Heaven, my Treasure Thou art.*
5. *High King of Heaven, my victory won, May I reach Heav'ns joys, O bright Heaven's Sun! Heart of my own heart, whatever befall, Still be my Vision, O Ruler of all.*

I literally put some of the words to the song on my board, as well as words like freedom, gratitude, enjoying God's abundance, and images of family, friends, and inspiring images of being fit etc. I know a lot of people use vision boards for manifesting the kind of car they want to drive or house they want to have. Although I had never had a vision board before, I have done this in the past with a home that we wanted to purchase. It was a villa in Vermont originally priced at over 2 million dollars. I put a photo of the house on a corkboard with a price written on it of $850,000. And do you know, we purchased that house for that amount! At the time, my husband and I were not even thirty years old. I had recently finished graduate school with a master's in public health, and I thought I would be working in the developing world or inner cities, helping to fight infectious disease.

In order to make money, however, we had started selling books on the internet. We were starting to do well with our business and were voracious savers. We had paid off our first home and had saved a good amount for a down payment on this "dream villa" that was in the town that we lived in. We had traveled a lot and loved Italy and good architecture. This house had been built by an Italian opera singer, and opera was also a love of ours. The pieces just kept fitting together.

While we enjoyed our time in that home, I started down the slippery slide of taking my eyes off God and onto myself. We were making more and more money, but I was falling further from my faith. Even amid all the parties I was throwing and the fun we were having, my mission of helping the poor was no longer in focus because God was no longer at the center.

You see, God will sometimes give us the desires of our hearts, even though they are not the desires of His heart. He wants us to have faith for big things. When we were buying the house, I thought originally maybe we could have it as a home for foster children or some other beneficial purpose, but my resolve was not that strong. He uses these things to test us and see our motivations. I sadly must admit I failed that test.

I want to pause for a moment to share an old Chinese story called *The Magic Paintbrush.*[15] The story tells of a young boy who was kind but very poor. He loved to draw, and in various versions he either meets an old man who gives him a magic paintbrush or dreams of the paintbrush and then it appears when he wakes up. The paintbrush can make whatever he draws become real, so he uses the paintbrush for good to help the poor around him by drawing, for example, a river where they can get water or food for them to eat. One day, however, a greedy man in the village forced the boy to draw him a mountain of gold. The boy was smart, however, and first drew a sea around the mountain, so that the man would have to sail far away to get the gold. He drew him a boat, and as he was sailing to the mountain, the boy drew a powerful storm – and the man never came back. The boy then went back to being able to help the village with his drawings.

This story illustrates the point that we are all given a magic paintbrush with which we can paint our lives. God wants us to be co-creators with Him. It's better, however, when our vision is in line with His - a Godly vision… not a greedy one. When we use our paintbrush to help others, a beautiful world is created. So much of the pain in the world today comes from our selfish desires.

Many times, we can have blind spots in our vision that can lead to accidents as well. If we can figure out where our blind spots are then we can take more of an account for them. When driving, we have rear view and side mirrors to help us with these blind spots. While we need to live in the present, looking at our past (our rear view) can help us to get a better sense of where we are and what may come up to throw us off course. We only want to do this briefly, however, just like you don't drive with your eyes focused on the rear view. Our friends can also help us see our blind spots. If you have other passengers in your car and you start to move into another lane with a car coming up that you didn't see, the other passengers will usually quickly tell you of your mistake. We now have special tools in our cars that can help us with this as well. We can't all have 100% vision all the time, but if we have people or tools to help guide us, then we can go the path that we are meant to travel.

On this journey of life, we need to have focus to be able to see the things that might come our way. To continue with the driving analogy, most of the accidents that happen on the road result from not being able to focus and not being able to react properly. This might be caused from being intoxicated or on drugs, from being distracted, or from being sleepy. While substance abuse will certainly take away your focus, I would have to guess that most of us lose our focus due to distractions. Just like we shouldn't be texting and driving, we need to look to see how many times we have our eyes glued on our phones or tablets when our children are trying to speak to us. If you take a moment to look around you some time when you are at an airport or even a restaurant, see how many of us have our eyes buried in some form of technology.

The character of Wonder Woman, the hero from the movies, needs to be alert and focused at all times to be on guard. Proverbs 4:23 says, "Above all else, guard your heart, for everything you do flows from it." Also, in Matthew 6: 19-23, it says this:

"Do not store up for yourselves treasures on earth, where moths and vermin destroy, and where thieves break in and steal. But store up for yourselves treasures in heaven, where moths and vermin do not destroy, and where thieves do not break in and steal. For where your treasure is, there your heart will be also. "The eye is the lamp of the body. If your eyes are healthy, your whole body will be full of light. But if your eyes are unhealthy, your whole body will be full of darkness. If then the light within you is darkness, how great is that darkness!

We need healthy eyes to be able to properly see and guard our treasure. If our treasure is anything outside of ourselves, we run the risk of it being destroyed, which is why the song says, "Thou and Thou only, first in my heart High King of Heaven, my Treasure Thou art." We need to keep our focus on God and the training He is preparing us for here in this game of life on earth. The definition of focus is a center of activity, attraction, or attention. We need to pay attention and get rid of distraction. Athletes who need focus and precision for their sport practice repeatedly, which is how they gain traction, and we need to do this daily too. Traction is defined as the grip of a tire on a road or a wheel on a rail. A car that is stuck in a sand pit, can't move forward because the wheels have no traction. The word dis-traction literally means the inability to move forward. This is why I was feeling like a hamster on a wheel, feeling a little stuck due to all the shiny distractions that kept appearing. As my vision was getting clearer, I was starting to realize that the traction I thought I was making was just false traction.

It's interesting when I look at my vision board now because I had literally clipped from a magazine the words, "What does slow living mean to you?" (Little did I know how slow things would get?) When you watch movies of superheroes, they often convey the quickness of the hero's acute vision in dodging the bullets or arrows as being in slow motion. When we think of focus, the image that comes to mind for me is an arrow and a target. A target is made up of concentric circles and the obvious goal is to hit the center mark. An archer must have extreme concentration to get his or her body in alignment with the target. By concentrating and slowing down, people have said that they experienced time in a different way. The common Greek word for sin used in the New Testament is *hamartia.* This word derives from a technical word used in archery, which literally means to miss the mark. Now, many people might hear this and think that if they ever mess up and don't hit their goals that it is a sin, but that's not what it means. It means that when we sin, or break the spiritual laws, it causes us to be out of alignment with our focus on our ultimate goal of spiritual reunion.

God wants to lead each of us on a journey. He wants to guide us and give us "supervision" if we let him. He knows our path from start to finish, so isn't it better if we are aligned with One who can "oversee" our lives? If you have never read the book, *Pilgrim's Progress*,[16] by John Bunyan, I encourage you to do so. It's an oldie (literally from 1698) but a goodie. It's an allegory of the Christian faith, where a man, aptly named Christian, leaves the "City of Destruction" and goes on a journey to the Celestial City, known as Mount Zion. Along the way, just like in our own lives, he finds there are distractions, gets stuck, leaves his burdens at the foot of the cross, and eventually makes "progress." If you too, want to make progress toward the things and places that God has planned for you, you need to learn to follow the signs that he has posted and listen to the guides that have been placed in your life. In the next chapter, we will explore that more together.

Reflection Questions for Journaling or Group Discussion

- What is your vision for the future? Does it line up with your values? Make a date with yourself or friends to create a new vision board of your life as a Wonder Woman.

___

___

___

- What are some things that can take away your focus or give you blind spots?

___

___

___

- If you want to have super vision for your life, in what ways do you need to allow God to have "supervision" over your life?

___

___

___

Chapter Eight: A Wonder Woman Knows Where She's Going

I find the great thing in this world is not so much where we stand, as in what direction we are moving: To reach the port of heaven, we must sail sometimes with the wind and sometimes against it - but we must sail, and not drift, nor lie at anchor.
– Oliver Wendell Holmes Jr.

Many times, we have goals, and we work towards achieving them only to find it was the wrong goal. We've all heard those stories about soccer players kicking the ball into their own goal post, basketball players making a huge dunk into their own basket, or football players running an amazing touchdown - only to hear that awful truth that they were running the wrong way. The elation they felt in those moments of what they thought was achievement, turns into years of embarrassment and humiliation. We've probably all heard that Lily Tomlin quote, "the problem with the rat race is that at the end of the day, you're still just a rat." As we climb the ladders of success, we need to make sure our ladder is in the right place; otherwise, we'll get to the top and realize there's nothing there or that what we were searching for doesn't satisfy. We need to head in the right direction, run the right race, and climb the right ladder.

For years I have been tracking goals using a website called the Day Zero Project (www.dayzeroproject.com). The idea is to try to achieve 101 goals in 1,001 days. There are even all kinds of ideas for goals on there if you don't have goals of your own. You can look at what other people's goals are and categorize your goals into current, ongoing, someday, and done. When I look at my list, I've accomplished thousands of goals. They can be as simple as 'go on a picnic' or 'stargaze' or as lofty as 'buy my own home' or 'graduate with honors.' It's fun to see how many things you've done in your life because it gives you a sense of accomplishment and pride and also motivates you to check things off your list.

Unfortunately, I've realized that many of these goals I was setting for myself were taking me in a different direction than my dreams. These goals are more like desires. There's a subtle, but important difference between desires and dreams. Desires are things we want - cravings that can leave us just wanting more. The Buddhists call desire the root of all suffering. We want, and we don't have, which leads us to feel incomplete without that thing. Then, once we have that one thing that we thought would make us so happy, we wake up one day to find it hasn't filled that void - and we're on to the next desire.

In the movie, *The Gods Must Be Crazy*,[17] an empty glass soda bottle accidentally falls from an airplane onto an African village who has not been exposed yet to the Western world. At first the item makes the villagers happy. They find all kinds of uses for it, but eventually they start fighting over it - greedy for their turn. It's a lighthearted, comical movie which illustrates how easily our desire for something causes suffering.

Going back to the Day Zero Project, although the site itself can be a very useful tool, I have realized how my goals were merely desires. I would spend precious time and energy to achieve a goal that was mistakenly headed in the opposite direction of my dreams. Dreams are big ideas that should, I think, ultimately make the world a better place. Our night dreams help us to make sense of the world in our sleep as our bodies repair any damage that has been done during the day. The best dreams we can set for ourselves are ones that do the same for our world - ones that help us make sense of the chaos and that heal our brokenness. I've had dreams that help to do this for a long time, but I got distracted chasing after small desires. Best-selling author, Rachel Hollis[18] has explained goal setting and dreams in a very visual way. She says you can either kick a ball ten times in one direction toward your goal or you can kick ten balls in ten different directions. You're using the same amount of time and energy.

While I can brag that I have done some incredible things, many of these goals have gotten me exactly to zero. While the name of the site implies counting down the days left to accomplish goals, for me it's a different kind of zero. Ecclesiastes 1:14 says, "I have seen all things that are done under the sun; all of them are meaningless, a chasing after the wind."

y for me, the game isn't over, and I have a chance · I started going in the wrong direction and get toward the right goals. If you feel like this, you can too. This is why it is important to measure goals - to see how far you've come. When we measure length, we use a ruler. It's interesting that we use the same word for a measuring stick as we do for a governing entity or authority. A ruler is a guide that helps us know what the rules are. I know many people in today's world say to do whatever you want or believe whatever you want. The thing about a game though is that it wouldn't be much fun if we all played by different rules. Imagine how that soccer game would turn out. It would be chaos. Likewise, imagine if your house was built by different carpenters who used differing measuring units. Do you think you would have much confidence in the integrity of the structure? I don't think I would sleep very well at night.

The word integrity has an interesting definition: it can mean "the state of being whole and undivided" and also "the quality of being honest and having strong moral principles; moral uprightness." It's related and comes from the word *integer*, which means a whole number. One of our most fundamental human desires is our need to be whole and to have what we think about ourselves in our mind equal to reality or how others perceive us. So many of our failures to live a life of integrity come from a lack of wholeness. We try to fill the "holes" with so many other things instead of being in alignment with the ruler. If only we would model the holiness of God, our holes would be transformed into a life of wholeness.

The universe has been given a number of physical rules that we know always exist. How would you feel if one day gravity just disappeared, or the sun didn't shine? Rules give our world stability, and therefore freedom to move about without worrying about it. As scientists learn and discover the rules that govern the physical world, the more inventions they can create and the farther forward we are able to move with technology. The spiritual rules for the game of life have been given to us as well. As we research and understand these laws more deeply, we can, just like technology, use these to transform and change our lives.

Scientists have developed GPS (Global Positioning Systems) to help guide us where we want to go, and we all understand how much value and time it saves us each day. GPS works by helping us know where we are by assessing our position in the world. It constantly monitors where we are and gives us feedback. When we have gone the wrong way or missed our turn, it gives us guidance, such as "make a U-turn." Our conscience is our internal GPS (or God Positioning System) that tells us if we are going in the right direction. We can choose to ignore it, but if we do, we may get stuck in "traffic."

1 Timothy 1:19 says, "Cling to your faith in Christ, and keep your conscience clear. For some people have deliberately violated their consciences; as a result, their faith has been shipwrecked." To be shipwrecked is an awful state to be in - lost, hungry, and perhaps alone. We've all read or seen movies of shipwrecks, and yet miraculously some of these people are saved. If you feel shipwrecked in your faith or know someone who has been, all is not lost, but you're going to need to call out for help. God has had a lot of practice in rescuing His children!

Wherever you are in this moment, you can take an honest assessment of where you are, where you've been and where you want to go. Sometimes we can get stuck looking at the past, thinking that we've made too many mistakes. But this just keeps you stuck. We don't always know why our path has led a certain way, but we can have faith that there can be a destiny in the detour as well. Life has many lessons to teach us. I personally know that I had to experience all the things in my path - the good, the bad, and the ugly - to make me into the Wonder Woman I am. I know the same is true for you if you are willing to learn the lessons you've been given.

In school, if you haven't learned the lessons properly, they don't advance you to the next grade. They are really doing a disservice if they do just move you along. You must learn basic addition before you can do multiplication and you must learn multiplication before you can do advanced material. Maybe you don't like math, so maybe that's a bad example - but think about whatever field you're in or studied and something you enjoyed. You weren't just thrown into a field without training. I wouldn't hire an electrician who hadn't passed an exam or go to a salon who hired people who just *thought* they'd like to cut hair for a living.

The school or game of life isn't quite as obvious in its training. You can't sign up for a class - but you can learn to recognize when a lesson presents itself and be willing to learn from those who have been through those lessons. As you start moving forward, you will go through progressively higher and higher levels, kind of like a video game. The challenges will be more difficult as you go, but the rewards will also be greater. Unlike a video game, you don't die if you make a mistake. Our mistakes can often be our best teachers, and there are thousands of examples of amazing men and women throughout history who persevered through thousands of mistakes to finally accomplish their goals. There's a song from the old movie, *Chitty Chitty Bang Bang*, that says, "From the ashes of disaster grow the roses of success."[19] If you feel like your life up until this point has been a disaster or that you've made too many mistakes, that just means you are in the perfect position to succeed. You now have great soil to produce the blooms that you desire if you will just realize this and "bloom where you're planted."

Also, if you feel like you have been in a pit, just remember that the pitstop is necessary in a race and it's a perfect time for a change. When cars race, they must stop in the pit to get re-oiled and change whatever tires or things need to be changed. But don't stay in the pit. You've got to get back into the race and head in the right direction. If you're ready to move, you'll have to do some planning and preparation.

Reflection Questions for Journaling or Group Discussion

- What goals do you have that are really just desires distracting you from an ultimate dream?

  ____

  ____

  ____

- What holes do you have in your life that are keeping you from experiencing wholeness?

  ____

  ____

  ____

- Take some time to be still and listen to your internal GPS. Are you headed in the right direction or where may you have gotten off course?

  ____

  ____

  ____

CHAPTER *Nine:* A WONDER WOMAN PREPARES

"By failing to prepare, you are preparing to fail." — Benjamin Franklin

A hero isn't a hero unless they've been through a battle or proved themselves in some way. But no one wants to go into a battle unprepared. Over the next few chapters, we'll discuss how a wonder woman trains and some of the things she takes into battle. You may be thinking to yourself at this point that you thought this book was all about bringing the wonder and joy back into your life. How are we now talking about battles and training?

The thing is that battles are coming whether we want them or not. There are forces in the universe that want to keep you from discovering your true identity. They know how strong and powerful you could be, and they like things as the status quo. In this world there are many advertisers who have an interest in keeping you stuck, so that you keep coming back to buy their products. If you know the history of indentured servitude or sharecroppers, many landlords through time have kept people feeling trapped in a cycle of slavery by limiting the number of supplies they had access to and overcharging them. While we are by no means limited any longer to our access to physical supplies in the material world, we must ask ourselves the question: if we are free, why don't we always feel free? We need to ask ourselves what we are being limited by. While many battles in the physical world are over money and power, many more of our battles come from a desire for freedom - either for ourselves or others.

In our fast-paced world, there are so many forces fighting for our attention, and we need to be prepared for this. We're surrounded by a constant barrage from the media telling us what to believe and what to be afraid of. It used to be that if the person on tv said "breaking news," it actually meant something. Now they say it even if it is something that is not even newsworthy. During the pandemic of 2020 the use of the word "unprecedented" was, frankly, quite unprecedented. Seriously, pay attention to whatever news source you watch to see how many times in 30 minutes that they use words like these. Write them down. No matter what the current crisis is, I'm sure there's some "crisis" going on at the time you read this. How on earth are you supposed to feel free to fly or be full of wonder when you are under constant attack from the media that conveys to you that you should live as a slave to fear or that leaves you feeling in despair as you compare yourself to a photoshopped supermodel? They want you to feel that you will only be good enough if you have the shiniest toys or the nicest home. They want you to feel you are loved only if you have a huge diamond to show it. They don't want you to realize that you *already are enough*, and *you have enough*.

Although the things of matter tempt us with promises of joy and happiness, they are often the very things that steal our joy. In Marie Kondo's book, *The Life Changing Magic of Tidying Up,*[20] she helps her readers see that they should only keep the items that truly bring them joy. While many view her methods as extreme, sometimes extreme situations call for extreme measures. Never in the history of the world have we ever been bogged down by so much stuff. Hoarding is a serious problem with serious consequences, with people literally feeling trapped by the material world. If you or someone you love suffers from tendencies to hoard, there are many people you can turn to who can help you professionally. Cleaning out cannot just be done physically, but a mental and spiritual cleansing needs to take place in the lives of those suffering from this "dis-ease".

When we live in an environment free from clutter, it also frees our minds and invites a spirit of freedom into our lives. I encourage you to read Marie Kondo's book because it truly will change your life. You need to create space for wonder and it's more difficult to create the space if you've cluttered your drawers with useless things. To create a meaningful life, keep the meaningful things sacred and don't surround them with junk. Just like I talked previously about detoxing your body and doing fasts, you also need to detox from your stuff. This can be done over the course of a weekend or longer if needed you can do it multiple times and in stages. In whatever way it best fits your life, find time to physically clear the clutter. The word clutter is a variant of *clotern*, which means "to form clots." Clots are blockages in your body that can lead to death. As you remove the blockages that don't give you joy, you will find space for the things that do. You want to create a space that inspires you. To inspire means "to breathe," so by creating that space in even just one room, means that you are allowing yourself a place to be free to breathe and live. Whatever size room or space you have, start there. You don't need to get bogged down by looking at magazines or desiring more stuff to fill the space. Magazines and Pinterest boards can definitely be "inspiring," but just make sure that what you are bringing into your home is well thought out and intentional.

It's always fun to watch shows or read blogs about people who transform homes. It's amazing to see how people can create something so beautiful out of something ugly. This transformation doesn't just happen overnight though. There is a lot of planning and preparation that goes into remodeling a house before the work even begins. I've restored four houses so far in my life, and each one has taught me invaluable things. It has not only taught me on-site electrical, plumbing, carpentry, painting, and design skills, but it has shown me the process and power of restoration. The first thing in any restoration process is the demolition. It's the removal of all the stuff that you don't like. You can't add the features you want until you take away the features you don't want. It's dirty and hard and sometimes also quite fun. I remember that first day when we bought our first 1700's Vermont colonial home. We got to work tearing off that old floral wallpaper like it was no one's business. It felt so good to be free of it. But then came the day- to-day work of scraping and plastering and sanding and painting. Each day brought us closer and closer to our goal, but we had to keep persisting for a long time.

I want you to think of yourself as a home or temple (which is what you are). To restore the wonder in yourself, allow God to be the architect of your life. As the owner of your home, you can give the architect your dreams and desires and what you want to see in your home, and then let God draw the plans He has for you. Unlike natural plans, however, we can't see them all spread out before us. We must do some work in the *natural*, to begin to see the *super-natural* plans revealed. We are going to begin that process by removing the features and things that we don't want in our home.

This is not just a one-day spring cleaning, however. Preparing your mind and spirit to be free is something that needs to occur intentionally and habitually. There are many books written about habits, and I encourage you to read one because habits create the *moments* of your life, and your moments create your *momentum*. I recommend *The Power of Habit*[21] by Charles Duhigg. Most of what we do in life is done unconsciously. We go through life many times not even aware of why we do the things we do. This is why it is so important to change our habits into intentional ones. When we look at the word *in-tend*, we see that it means to tend the inner parts of ourselves. The word tend is defined as regularly or frequently behaving in a particular way or to have certain characteristics. It can also mean to go or move in a particular direction, like saying the road tends east and down into the valley. Finally, it can mean to care for, to look after, or give one's attention to. Its really all the same definition though. Whatever we give our attention to is the direction we will go in or the particular way we will behave.

When I think of the word tend, my mind immediately thinks of gardening. I love to garden, and I encourage anyone who wants to experience more wonder, to care for plants. When you have plants, you must pay attention. The health of your plants can be a good indicator of how *wonder-full* you are feeling. It's like the idea of bringing a canary into a coal mine. Although gruesome, miners would bring a canary with them because if there were dangerous gases it would kill the canary first. It was their warning sign. If you're too busy to care for the plants, perhaps there are other things you are not tending to as well. The evidence of how we tend our lives don't always show up as quickly, but plants will show browning leaves or discoloration if they're not getting enough attention.

When we planted our vineyard, it taught me a lot about tending to vines. If you have a vine, you must train it to climb in a certain direction because once it has matured, the tender young vine (see that word again) will harden into more of a bark that is sturdy and strong and can support the other growing parts of itself. Initially, a grape plant will send shoots out in all directions in a tangled mess. It's up to the vineyard keeper to trim off the chutes and keep just the most upright and healthiest chute. That one will be trained to climb the trellis and be guided along the wires.

It is so important to cut out the things from your life that aren't serving you because it's training the best parts of you to go in the right direction. To have a strong plant, you also need to pull the weeds, nourish it with good nutrients and water, and keep the pests away. When we planted our vineyard, we went just a little overboard and planted 150 plants! We had 15 acres, so we naively wanted a certain "look." The problem with that was that it meant 150 plants that needed to be trained and staked and 150 plants that needed weeding and pest management. Even though we put down weed blocking material, they popped through because we just couldn't keep up with it or the pest attacks. I learned an important lesson that less is sometimes more. If we had concentrated on fewer plants, we could have likely produced more fruit.

By "weeding" out the stuff around us, it can cause us to have the space to really grow. If you feel like you are constantly spending too much time doing laundry, perhaps look at how many clothes you have. Before you toss something in the basket, ask yourself if it is truly dirty. We particularly must teach our kids how to do this. Better yet, if you have kids old enough to dress themselves, you probably have kids old enough to help do the laundry. This will help them to think twice before they throw something in the basket, just because it's easier than putting it in the drawer.

I know at the beginning of this chapter, we said we were going to be preparing for battles, so you may be wondering how this relates to clutter clearing, gardening, and house restoration analogies. While physical training of your body is important and we will talk about this later, I wanted to first get down to the basics. I've never been in the military, but I know in bootcamp training, a big part of it is breaking you down. Like a muscle must break apart in order to build it stronger, the first thing we need to do is break free and break away from the things that are limiting you. Clearing clutter may not seem very important, but I assure you it's an integral step in beginning your preparation. It's the demolition part of the house restoration process or the tilling of the soil in our garden analogy. It is preparing you for something more and it's breaking you free from the things that you think "matter" so that we can see beyond this natural world into the supernatural.

When you watch movies of some hero being given instruction by a master, the master always seems to give the hero a trivial task at the beginning, which the student is frustrated by.

The student complains to the master that it doesn't seem like that thing would really help in their fight. But then, little by little, they learned by repetitive motions to transform themselves into a warrior. The master knows the journey because he's been there. As the old Chinese Proverb says, "A journey of a thousand miles begins with a single step." We must learn to listen to the Master's calling. Next, we will learn to develop those listening skills.

Reflection Questions for Journaling or Group Discussion

- What are the false limiting belief systems that keep you from living in freedom?

  ___

  ___

  ___

- Does your living space inspire you and give you room to breathe? If not, write down some simple things that you can do to create more breathing room, even if its just cleaning out a closet or donating some items you haven't used in years.

  ___

  ___

  ___

- Are there things that you should cut out from your life that aren't serving you? Are you tending to the most important things and training your life to go in a certain way or are you being pulled in too many directions?

  ___

  ___

  ___

CHAPTER Ten:

A WONDER WOMAN HAS SUPER HEARING

We need to find God, and he cannot be found in noise and restlessness. God is the friend of silence. See how nature - trees, flowers, grass- grows in silence; see the stars, the moon and the sun, how they move in silence... We need silence to be able to touch souls. – Mother Teresa

When you think of a superhero from the movies, you often think of them rescuing people in trouble. Somehow, they can hear a person's cry for help from miles away. We need to train our ears to hear the messages that are being sent to us. Everything (literally everything) in life comes from vibration, but we can understand this best when it comes to sound. We see how we beat on a drum or play a piano and the vibration of that instrument is heard on our eardrums. We can hear clearly if we are close to an object, but if we put up barriers like a wall between us and the source of the sound, the harder it is to hear. The sound waves are blocked by the barrier, and we hear in a more limited way or not at all.

In the Bible in 1 Kings 19: 11 - 13, a story is told about God speaking to the Prophet Elijah. It says, "The Lord said, 'Go out and stand on the mountain in the presence of the Lord, for the Lord is about to pass by.' Then a great and powerful wind tore the mountains apart and shattered the rocks before the Lord, but the Lord was not in the wind. After the wind there was an earthquake, but the Lord was not in the earthquake. After the earthquake came a fire, but the Lord was not in the fire. And after the fire came a gentle whisper. When Elijah heard it, he pulled his cloak over his face and went out and stood at the mouth of the cave."

God was showing up in a whisper, or a *still small voice*, as it says in other translations, which means you must be quiet or *still* in order to hear it. There are barriers all around you. We live in such a noisy world that the term "noise pollution" is a common phrase. When was the last time you were utterly quiet? Even if it has been a long time, you can probably vividly recall the awe and reverence you felt for that moment. It likely felt wonder-full. In our everyday lives, we live with noise around us. Crying babies and honking horns are there to serve a purpose – they get our attention if there is an urgent need. While some people choose a life of quietness as a nun or monk, or like Thoreau who lived intentionally in the woods near Walden Pond, many of us have already chosen a different path. Although we can't just abandon our partners, children, or responsibilities to live a life of quiet, we can start training ourselves to add times of quietness into our lives every day.

If you have children, this can be particularly difficult to find. They are growing humans and seem to constantly be hungry or need something of you. While I have never been a morning person, I have had to train myself to wake early (ie. 5am) – before the kids get up. This is not easy to do and will take time to make it into a routine – but trust me – it has fundamentally altered my ability to hear and to have the stillness I need to experience the wonder. Most of this book was written during this time of day if that tells you anything.

Creating a good morning routine has been written about by many successful people. Why do they all share this same habit? It has to do with your brain waves and the correlation between the frequency of those waves and the body's state when waking. When you first awake, your brain operates predominantly in the alpha wave, which has been called the gateway to the subconscious mind. When you wake up early and in peace, the mind is capable of deep and profound learning and focus. At this time, your mind is very impressionable, so whatever you do or are exposed to, sets the tone for your entire day. I'm not sure it matters exactly what time you get up, although some people swear that certain hours are better than others. The thing that most people agree on though is that meditation, prayer, journaling, affirmations, and the like are crucial when you first get up. The worst thing you can do is grab your phone, start checking social media or the news, or get woken up by a child wanting their breakfast. If you have children and they get up early, it just means you'll need to set your alarm for an hour earlier. It may seem hard, but your future self will thank you for the investment.

I had been getting up early the last few years, but I wasn't aware of the importance of the first twenty minutes until recently. I used to use my phone as an alarm by my bed. The temptation with that is to check emails or social media as the first thing you do. It's also very easy to hit the snooze button if it's too close to the bed. Having to get up and go into another room creates momentum for me. Even if I'm tired, I'm not going to crawl back into bed at that point. It motivates me to put the tea pot on and have my quiet time.

Have you ever been to a science museum where they demonstrate how sound travels? They usually have some kind of large wall or curved piece, and they tell you that if you put your ear in just the right place and if your friend goes to the other side and whispers into another spot they have designated, you can hear your friend's whisper. This demonstrates the fact that sound is traveling in ways we cannot perceive, but that you must be in the right position to hear it. By waking early and clearing away the distractions, you are putting yourself in a better position to hear from the Spirit. Many people recommend putting yourself into a physical position as well. If I were to lie flat on my back when I first wake up and try to meditate, I would be back to sleep before I knew it. You must physically move and change your position, whether you get down on your knees, prostrate yourself on the floor, sit in a yoga pose, or do what you feel led to do. Sometimes you can hear better on a run or in the shower. Wherever it is, it is usually a time where your mind is free and can receive the messages.

Think of your mind as a wave receiver. Radio waves have always existed since the beginning of time, but it was not until the end of the 19th century that we learned how to use them. We take radio for granted now but imagine being the first people to hear a radio broadcast. You could be in California and hear what was going on in New York City just by having this radio device in your living room. It's mind boggling when you really think about how our technology has advanced by harnessing the power of waves. Our cell phones transmit messages to us instantaneously. It doesn't matter how far away your friend is on the other end, you can usually hear them like they are in the same room as you. Have you ever stopped to just appreciate and wonder at the marvels of all the things we use every day?

Prayer is an even more advanced technology than our cell phones because unlike our phones, which can be dropped and broken, prayer is harnessing the power of sound waves using the amazing computer that is your mind. There are billions of stories of answered prayers. We call it miraculous because we don't understand this amazing power, just like if you could go back in time and brought a cell phone into the time of Shakespeare. The people would think it was miraculous. Prayer is not just something we say before we eat dinner or a list of items that we want God to do for us. It is an untapped technology that has been known to us for a long time, and yet to master it requires practice. Mother Teresa said, "I always begin my prayer in silence, for it is in the silence of the heart that God speaks. God is the friend of silence-we need to listen to God because it's not what we say but what He says to us and through us that matters."

There are countless stories of people who've heard from God and obeyed, and miracles ensued. The Holy Spirit wants to use us to be the hands and feet of the miraculous and wonderful works. Perhaps someone needs a certain amount of money to pay rent. There are many accounts of times when someone else has heard the Spirit telling them the exact amount and who to give it to. Or other stories of, for example, people who felt a nudge to visit an aunt only to find that she had collapsed on the floor and couldn't call for help. While anecdotal narratives may not sound like proof of the power of prayer, when it has happened billions of times, it is something that can't be ignored.

The thing about a phone is that you must answer it. If you receive a call with an urgent message, you can choose to ignore it - but then whose fault is it if you didn't hear it? We must train our minds to be connected to the incoming signals. I often wear a Bluetooth headset when I want to listen to an audio book. It's a good way to feed my mind while doing laundry or dishes or making dinner. I can listen to the book easily and have my hands free. The thing about it though, is that I must stay in a certain range to my phone for it to work. If I get too far away, it clearly speaks to me and says, "disconnected." When I come closer and back into a position where it can connect, it says into my ear, "connected."

We need to be connected and in position for our minds to receive the signals that Spirit is trying to convey to us. We all know that there are many sounds that we cannot hear with our human ears. If you have a dog, or at least know how a dog whistle works, you know that dogs can hear at a higher frequency than humans can. Even children can hear at frequencies that adults cannot. As we age, our ability to perceive these frequencies diminishes. While we may not be able to reverse our age and hear these higher sounds again, the point that I want to show to you is that there are vibrations and waves all around us that we cannot sense in the natural world. While we may understand this in theory, we need to take a moment to really let that sink into our hearts. So often we think that what we see and hear with the senses is what is true. The reality is that there is so much more beyond our senses.

We also need to be careful of what we listen to. Words and music are extremely powerful. Just think about a time when just one or two words spoken by someone else have greatly impacted you, either positively or negatively. Words have the power to hurt or to heal. Be careful who you are allowing to speak into your life. The same can be true with music. The words that we allow into our minds through music can influence us more than we know. We all know how stupid jingles can get stuck on repeat in our brains.

Think about what you are currently listening to: is it lifting you up to become a wonder woman or dragging you down into a bad place? I challenge you to be intentional about your playlists. I know personally that if either my kids or I am starting to become negative or complain, I stop and put on an upbeat worship mix or a "growth mindset" mix for my kids. We start dancing and it stops the negativity in its tracks. Philippians 4:8 says, "Whatever is true, whatever is honorable, whatever is just, whatever is pure, whatever is lovely, whatever is commendable, if there is any excellence, if there is anything worthy of praise, think about these things." This is not just so that you can live a goody two-shoes life. That is not the point. The point is that your thoughts can become and manifest into the life you see around you, so you want to train your thoughts into being positive ones and attract the right things. If you want to learn to become attractive, keep reading.

Reflection Questions for Journaling or Group Discussion

- When was the last time you can remember being completely still and hearing the Spirit speak to you?

____

____

____

- Does your morning routine currently set you up for success, or do you start the day with distraction? If your cell phone is currently on your nightstand, start today by placing it in another room to charge.

____

____

____

- What words or songs have you allowed into your life that need to be removed? Come up with two practical ways to either remove negative influences or crowd them out with positive ones.

____

____

____

CHAPTER Eleven:

A WONDER WOMAN IS MAGNETIC

"Ask, and it will be given to you; seek, and you will find; knock, and it will be opened to you. For everyone who asks receives, and he who seeks finds, and to him who knocks it will be opened." – Matthew 7:7-8

When you think of a magnet, your mind probably immediately thinks of something you played with as a kid at home or in school or something you put on your refrigerator to hold up pictures. We all know that like attracts like and opposites repel. Picture in your mind holding those two sides of the magnet in your hands and feeling what it was like for those forces to come together or repel each other. The thing that we often forget is that there is magnetic energy all around us. The reason a compass works is because the powerful force of the magnetism points the metal towards the magnetic north pole. The magnetic field of the earth is the field that protects us from the powerful rays of the sun. When solar flares hit our earth, the magnetic field vibrates and if you are close enough to the poles you can visibly see our magnetic field as the Aurora Borealis or Australis.

While magnetism is something we can visibly see with our eyes, what I really want to talk about in this chapter is that invisible quality of what it means to be attractive. If I had said "A Wonder Woman is Attractive" as the title chapter, it may have turned some people away at first glance though. I didn't want anyone to feel that I was talking about physical attraction. While the character of *Wonder Woman* from the comic books and movies is physically attractive, to some extent we can't control the looks we were born with. This chapter is not about having a supermodel body or fitting into some stereotypical mold. What I want us to discover in this chapter is how we can be more attractive in other ways.

Much of what is attractive about someone comes not from their physical beauty, but from an inner confidence. In the movie *I Feel Pretty,*[22] the comedian Amy Schumer hits her head during an exercise class and wakes up thinking that she has been somehow transformed into a supermodel. Although everyone else sees her the same in her physical body, her confidence level skyrocketed and, although I don't want to give away the ending if you haven't seen it, you can imagine how this changed her life for the better.

That is the power of confidence. The word literally means "to have full trust or faith." Hebrews 11:1 says, "Now faith is confidence in what we hope for and assurance about what we do not see." There is a reason that the Bible is full of stories about faith. Faith is the key to life. The rest of the chapter goes on to say this:

This is what the ancients were commended for. By faith we understand that the universe was formed at God's command, so that what is seen was not made out of what was visible. By faith Abel brought God a better offering than Cain did. By faith he was commended as righteous, when God spoke well of his offerings. And by faith Abel still speaks, even though he is dead. By faith Enoch was taken from this life, so that he did not experience death: "He could not be found, because God had taken him away." For before he was taken, he was commended as one who pleased God. And without faith it is impossible to please God, because anyone who comes to him must believe that he exists and that he rewards those who earnestly seek him. By faith Noah, when warned about things not yet seen, in holy fear built an ark to save his family. By his faith he condemned the world and became heir of the righteousness that is in keeping with faith. By faith Abraham, when called to go to a place he would later receive as his inheritance, obeyed and went, even though he did not know where he was going. By faith he made his home in the promised land like a stranger in a foreign country; he lived in tents, as did Isaac and Jacob, who were heirs with him of the same promise. For he was looking forward to the city with foundations, whose architect and builder is God. And by faith even Sarah, who was past childbearing age, was enabled to bear children because she considered him faithful who had made the promise. And so from this one man, and he as good as dead, came descendants as numerous as the stars in the sky and as countless as the sand on the seashore.

I love this chapter because it's like the Cliff Notes of the Old Testament. I studied the Bible in school and grew up hearing about these stories of faith, but I know not everyone has had this opportunity. I like to direct people to read Hebrews 11 because it's like the trailer for the movie. If you want to know what the Old Testament is all about, this may wet your whistle to delve deeper. A testament is defined as "something that serves as a sign or evidence of a specified fact, event, or quality." The Bible is a written witness of the evidence of "things unseen." I want to bring our attention back to verse three: "By faith we understand that the universe was formed at God's command, so that what is seen was not made out of what was visible."

How is the invisible made visible? God's voice. In Genesis 1, the creation story uses the words, "God said" repeatedly to show us that it was through invisible sound waves that the universe was manifested. (ie. God said, "Let there be light and there was light"). The energy that Moses met in the burning bush referred to itself as something that is translated as "I am that I am" or "I will be who I will be." Written in the Hebrew as YHWH, it's an indescribable energy, and in the Jewish faith you are not even allowed to say the name because it's too beyond us to comprehend. The Spirit of God probably chose the words "I am" because these are the best words that we can use to understand the concept of being present.

I believe the words I AM are powerful. When we say or think the words "I am," it sends out a vibration like an electromagnetic wave that attracts the things and life we have thought or spoken. Many books have been written about the power of positive thinking, and I will not reinvent the wheel here, but I want to connect it back to wonder. When you open yourself to wonder, it opens the doors of possibility and creation. If you are fixed in a mindset that things are as they are, then they will stay as they are, but when you free your mind to explore the infinite universe around you, you discover the unlimited potential. Children know this power. They are unlimited in their creation and imagination. If you state positive affirmations using the words I am, it allows your mind the ability to visualize and create new things.

It's not just saying these words that makes the difference though. If you say the words but have no faith in them that these things can come true, then you are sending out mixed messages into the universe. When we back our "I am" statements with a conviction of faith, wonder-full things happen. It has been shown that performance in any task that we are trying to accomplish can be changed by our belief that we are better or worse at it. Athletes use the power of imagery or imagination to achieve things that often seem humanly impossible. In 1954, it was thought impossible for a man to run a mile in less than four minutes, but Roger Bannister broke that barrier - and since then, over 1,000 people have been able to accomplish this feat. Knowing that something has been done before can give you the confidence as well to achieve something you want to do. Whatever you are looking to do or to attract into your life, find stories of people who have accomplished similar things. At one point they too were at the same place that you are now. You can find hope in knowing that at one point they too were unknowing whether their dreams would come true.

Having a positive and optimistic attitude can enhance every aspect of your life. People like to be around happy and grateful people. Sweet smelling and beautiful flowers attract both bees and humans to them due to their beautiful characteristics. As Wonder Women, we can attract amazing things into our lives by creating attractive qualities in our lives. One of the most important qualities we should all possess is gratitude. Being thankful sends messages both to God and to others that you are someone deserving of more. Do you like giving gifts to someone who is ungrateful or complains about the gift that is given? Of course not. You're less likely to give them something in the future. Being thankful for the life you currently have is one of the most important steps in showing that you can be accepting of more.

As you think about the things you want to attract, focus on your vision. Keep in mind the end goal or the "fruit" of what it is that you want in your life. Do you want joy, peace, or love? Most of us ultimately want these things, but what are we attracting to produce this? Most plants do particular things to attract the type of pollinator they want so that they can be fertilized and produce fruit and pass on their genetic material. They may have showy blooms, produce a fragrance, or grow in a particular area. Galatians 5: 22-23 says, "The fruit of the Spirit is love, joy, peace, forbearance, kindness, goodness, faithfulness, gentleness and self-control." This is the fruit or evidence that I want to show in my life. Fruit takes time to develop. It starts with a flower that is fertilized and then it takes time to produce.

Start small. Just like a seed doesn't become a tree overnight, it takes time for things to grow in your life. Sometimes we want big changes to happen fast. While this can happen occasionally, most of the time, we experience and attract the things we want to see in our lives through a gradual process. We can often look at others and see what seems to be a flower blooming overnight. In the plant world, flowers do often appear quickly, but we must understand that it took a lot of growth for that flower to get there. It took planting, fertilizing, and weeding to create a healthy plant with a healthy bloom.

If you want joy in your life, start with a smile. Do you know that just by smiling that you can be happier? Seriously. Try it. I want you to stop what you are doing and smile for just 10 seconds. How do you feel? The act of smiling literally sends neurotransmitters like dopamine, serotonin and endorphins into your body that can relieve stress, pain, and elevate your mood. While some people say just "fake it 'til you make it," you don't necessarily have to just fake your smile. Just find some simple things that give you joy and try to work them into each day. One of my daughter's school assignments during Covid quarantine was to make a "happiness jar." They decorated it and then wrote on colored paper with simple things that made them happy. The idea is then to pull one thing out every day to do to just add a little extra joy into each day. If you enjoy silly videos of animals doing things on YouTube, go ahead. Take some time for laughter. It really is the best medicine. I created my own happiness jar along with my daughter, and one of the things I wrote was having fresh flowers on the table. It's such a little thing, but now I try to plan for this on my shopping list and budget.

It's not just about you though. Studies have shown that doing things for others increases your overall joy and satisfaction in life. Too often we live in an "entertain me" culture. If we are entertained too much or give ourselves too many things, it can actually decrease our joy. Going back to the first chapter, remember that joy is often found in the unexpected. Although I like the flowers on my table, sometimes I'll intentionally go a week without them, so that I appreciate them even more when I have them. Many times, when we have something too often, we become entitled in having that thing and our joy is diminished. Can you think of an entitled person? The term "Karen" is often used in today's culture for a person who is entitled and mean. Although I don't like that word frankly because I feel bad for all the ladies out there named Karen who are sweet and kind, the fact that the title exists at all says a lot about our culture. Why are there so many entitled, unkind people out there?

If you have been blessed with much, how much more should you be a blessing to others? Luke 12:48 says, "From everyone who has been given much, much will be demanded; and from the one who has been entrusted with much, much more will be asked." If I have been blessed with much, how much more is my responsibility to share that love and blessing with those around me. The gift is meant to be passed on. A pastor I once heard said it this way: what if the postal person was supposed to deliver a gift to you, but decided to keep it for themselves? We all agree that this would be wrong. But how often do we take something that we are meant to simply be the delivery person for and keep it for ourselves? It's obviously not so cut and dry, but we all need to count our blessings, be grateful, and "pay it forward."

A big part of increasing your attractive power comes from training yourself to forgive and let go of judgement. Matthew 7: 1-5 says, "Do not judge, or you too will be judged. For in the same way you judge others, you will be judged, and with the measure you use, it will be measured to you. 'Why do you look at the speck of sawdust in your brother's eye and pay no attention to the plank in your own eye? How can you say to your brother, 'Let me take the speck out of your eye,' when all the time there is a plank in your own eye? You hypocrite, first take the plank out of your own eye, and then you will see clearly to remove the speck from your brother's eye." If we don't want to be judged, we need to release our judgement both of others and ourselves. Forgiveness and release of judgement are the ultimate keys to your freedom. We all want to be free – so why do we hold on to these things?

Dr. Caroline Leaf is a neuroscientist and author of books such as *Switch on Your Brain*[23] and *Think and Eat Yourself Smart.*[24]

She also does a 21 day "brain detox" where you can go through a course online. In this course, you choose a toxic thought that you have and, little by little, acknowledge the thought and replace it with a healthy thought. I did this detox because a friend has asked me to do it with her as a way of having accountability. I didn't think I had any particularly awful toxic thoughts, but I had recently heard about Gabrielle Bernstein's book, *Judgement Detox: Release the Beliefs That Hold You Back from Living a Better Life*[25], and felt that the Spirit was leading me to "detoxify" my judgement. I really thought of myself as a non-judgmental person.... I love people of all races, religions, and genders. When I started paying attention to my judgmental thoughts though – wow! I was judging all day long. I realized how much I judged my kids, I judged my husband, and I really judged myself. Love and compassion are the opposite of judgement, so when I found myself having the toxic judgmental thought, I would learn to replace it with a healthy thought. It's like weeding your garden – you must get rid of toxic plants so that the ones you want there can flourish. I began seeing noticeable changes in the amount of joy I was having as well, and those around me did too. My daughter even wrote sticky notes and put them all over me one day with words like, "best mommy ever" and "I am kind." Where, previously, they would see a well-intentioned, but often frustrated mama, they were seeing a transformation in me into the kind of Wonder Woman I wanted to be.

One analogy Bernstein gave in her book is that when judgmental thoughts come at you, it's like a wave. If you resist it, it can knock you down and take you out. You get caught up in your judgement and start to drown in it. But if you acknowledge it and dive under the wave, you come out on the other side and can have fun in the water. This got me thinking about rip tides. I live by the beach, so I often see the signs and flags for rip currents. If you are caught in a rip current, the instructions tell you to let it take you out into deeper water and then call for help or swim out and around it. If you resist it and try to swim against it, you can drown. Our egos tell us that we are strong enough to resist and to keep fighting, but the truth is that we need to do the very opposite of what might seem "natural." Growing up in New England, I learned early in driver's education, that if you get caught in a skid due to rain or snow, that you paradoxically need to turn into the skid in order to get out of it. Your natural inclination might be to turn your tires in the opposite direction, but to save yourself from an accident, you just need to go with the flow.

Many years ago, I read Mihaly Csikszentmihalyi's book called *Flow*,[26] in which he investigates a state of consciousness he called flow that can lead to the experience of deep enjoyment, creativity, and a total involvement with life. It's those moments when you get totally caught up with whatever task you are doing that you don't even notice how long you've been doing it. When we find things that we love to do, we're not worrying or judging what other people are doing. One of my favorite quotes of all times is by Vincent Van Gogh: "It is good to love many things, for therein lies the true strength, and whosoever loves much performs much, and can accomplish much, and what is done in love is well done." Love brings us into a state of flow with what we do and the people who surround us. We can choose love, which will attract more love and good things into our lives, or we can choose fear and attract more fear and negativity. Let's train ourselves to overcome the fear.

Reflection Questions for Journaling or Group Discussion

- In what ways are your thoughts attracting positive or negative things into your life?

  ____
  ____
  ____

- Take note today of any judgmental thoughts that arise in you today. Acknowledge the thought but try not to judge yourself for having the thought. Later on, write down why you think you might be having those thoughts and how you can change those thoughts to ones of acceptance.

  ____
  ____
  ____

- What gives you the most joy? What is it that feels more like play that also gives you a sense of purpose?

  ____
  ____
  ____

CHAPTER *Twelve:* A WONDER WOMAN OVERCOMES

"The most successful people see adversity not as a stumbling block, but as a stepping-stone to greatness." – Shawn Achor

To become a Wonder woman, we need to overcome the things that are holding us back. The word overcome literally means to "come over." Think of it like training for the hurdles race. In your path there will be obstacles you will face and fears that seem to loom large. You can't just stop there and wait to see if it will go away. You can't go back. You could probably find a way to go around it, but that would be cheating and not the point. You must train yourself to go over the hurdles.

The word over has many definitions depending on how you use it. It can be a verb, adjective, preposition, prefix, or adverb. Besides being a term in the game of cricket, however, it is never a noun. It is a state that requires action of some kind. The origin of the word comes from "ofer" or "ove," meaning above, higher than, or beyond, and is related to the word super. "Uffera" comes from the Old English, meaning past or finished - from beginning to end.

When we think about a superhero, we envision someone flying over the earth. A hurdle race would be nothing to them because they know how to go fast, and they know how to soar over the barriers. We often think the hurdles in our life look too large, but this is only because we are seeing ourselves as being too small. A caterpillar on the ground sees a stick across its path as a hurdle to get over, whereas we barely even notice it. Once that caterpillar becomes a butterfly, it won't notice it either. The hurdle that seemed so large before won't even be an issue.

If we want to overcome obstacles in our life, we can spend a lot of time training to beat the odds. I know from God's Word, though, that Christ has already beat the odds and declared "it is finished" or "it is over" on the cross. It's interesting how "ofer" sounds like "offering" - the perfect lamb who was slain for the sins of the world. At that moment, the veil of the temple was torn in two, signifying that God himself paid the price for our mistakes. Even before this moment, Jesus told his disciples, "I have told you these things so that you may have peace. In this world you will have trouble. But take heart! I have overcome the world." (John 16:33)

When we take on the identity that we are children of God, we undergo transformation. It makes us bigger and changes us into someone who sees the same obstacles in a very different way. Like a butterfly going through the stages of metamorphosis, we need to go through stages of development from a tiny egg into a caterpillar and then into a butterfly that can spread its wings and travel incredible distances. If you have ever had the privilege of seeing all these stages, it is truly miraculous to witness. During the first week of coronavirus homeschool quarantine, my daughter's second grade teacher went to each of her student's homes and dropped off milkweed plants that had monarch butterfly eggs on their leaves. The children were able to see and report on how the eggs hatched into tiny caterpillars and grew bigger until they formed their chrysalis and emerged as a butterfly. Our tiny plant had 21 caterpillars on it, which they demolished until there was nothing left. We had to get another plant and then they ate that too (talk about muchness!)

We often overlook this growth process when we think of metamorphosis. We think only of the butterfly emerging. Just like the caterpillars need to fill their stomachs to grow, we too need to fill our hearts and minds with spiritual food so that we can be strong enough to go through the process of transformation. John 6:35 says, "Then Jesus declared, "I am the bread of life. Whoever comes to me will never go hungry, and whoever believes in me will never be thirsty."

We were able to see two of them emerge from the chrysalis, which was breathtaking to watch. Sometimes we can look and see other wonderful women and become jealous. We forget the hard things they have overcome and the transformation that had to take place in their lives to get them to where they are. When a caterpillar makes its chrysalis, it doesn't just go in there, sleep, and come out with wings. That's not the way it works. What happens is that every single part of that caterpillar is broken down until it becomes like a liquid. Only then can the cells rearrange and create an entirely new state of being.

This is such a great analogy for us because it helps us to know that when everything is murky and nothing seems to make sense, this can often be the time of greatest transformation if we let it. Many people refer to this time as the dark night of the soul or various analogies of the kind. It feels hard to keep going when things seem dark, but the Spirit promises us that the Word of God will be a lamp unto our feet and a light unto our path. It doesn't say, the whole path will be shown to us. It's just enough light for the step we're on. That may be scary because we don't know what's out in the darkness, but that's how we overcome our fears.

My first job after graduating college was teaching outdoor education in the Redwood forests of California. (Can I just say Best. Job. Ever?) Part of the program involved taking the students on a night hike. Darkness can be scary for a lot of us because our brains go wild imagining all the kinds of fantasies that are not really there. If you have a flashlight, it at least helps you know where you're going. Well, part of this night hike always involved one part where we challenge the students to walk a very short straight and familiar part of the path by themselves without a flashlight. One of the leaders would go ahead and the students would take turns walking to us. It was only about 30 seconds, but the students often talked afterwards about this was one of their favorite things because, although they were afraid, they learned that there was nothing to fear, and they felt stronger and more confident after they did it.

The word fear is often referred to by the acronym "Face Everything and Rise" or another one is "False Evidence Appearing Real." It's good to be reminded of this because otherwise our fears can hold us captive in an imaginary prison of our own making. We all know stories of people with phobias who literally can't even live an ordinary life (let alone an extraordinary one) due to their fears.

We see others' fear sometimes as being silly, but we need to examine our own fears to make them vanish. When you shed light on darkness, the darkness disappears. When I was able to examine, for example, the root causes of my judgment, I discovered that I had toxic thoughts of perfectionism. Perfectionism comes from a fear of not being enough just as you are. I judged myself, my kids, and husband in this way, which affected how I would treat myself and them. When I looked at this closely, I realized it was impacting me in more ways than I knew. Perfectionism led me to feel overwhelmed sometimes in making decisions. Instead of just deciding something, I was trapped by a fear of making the wrong choice. Perfectionism can lead to a lack of self-confidence because of the self-conscious desire to never make a mistake. The thing is that mistakes are how we learn. When a child is learning to walk, they fall down many times. No loving parent ever scolds them for falling. They just encourage them to keep walking. The same is true with our heavenly Father.

The word "perfect" comes from the Latin "perfectus," which means "to complete." I have adopted this definition into my own life instead of the unattainable version of perfect that most of us have in our minds. When I think of being complete, I think of being whole and when I think about being whole, I think about being holy. God is holy and perfect. Matthew 5: 48 says "be perfect, even as your Father in heaven is perfect." We look at that and we think we might as well throw in the towel. How could I ever be perfect? When we understand that we are made *complete* due to the Spirits' love, we can step into that perfection. Notice that the verse says, "be perfect." It does not say "do perfectly." There is a big difference in being and doing. We are human beings… not human doings. When a caterpillar turns into a butterfly, it is simply being who it was created to be. It doesn't have to think about it too hard.

When driving a car we don't always need to put our foot on the gas to move forward. All we need to do is take our foot off the brake. Too often we are trying to move forward, but we have one foot on the metaphorical brake. Think of the gas pedal as having the word "action" on it and the brake as having other anti-action words on it: distr-action, re-action, dissatisf-action, fr-action, trans-action, inter-action etc. Even attr-action and satisf-action can keep you stalled if they are towards things that keep you from being wonder-full.

You already are endowed with powers and capabilities that should move you into an amazing journey. When we overcome the things holding us back, we be-come the person we were created to be. We overcome or "come over" to the other side of the rainbow where "skies are blue and the dreams that we dare to dream really do come true." *Somewhere Over the Rainbow*[27] was one of my favorite songs as a child, and I loved the "Wonderful" Wizard of Oz. It's a great metaphor for the journey of life. Even in Oz, things weren't "perfect," but they were at least colorful and exciting. Dorothy and her friends still had to overcome and defeat the "wicked witch." Through the journey, they were endowed with courage, a new heart, and a new mind (or brain). She ultimately returns home with some new insights.

In Joseph Campbell's groundbreaking work, *The Hero with a Thousand Faces,*[28] he shows us how almost every story and tale throughout history has similar features in it:

1. The call to adventure
2. The refusal of the call

3. Meeting the mentor
4. Crossing the threshold
5. Tests
6. Approaching the innermost cave
7. Ordeal
8. Reward/ Bliss
9. The Road back
10. Resurrection
11. Master of two worlds

If you think of any story you like, it can almost always be summarized into three parts - going away, being initiated, and coming back. There's usually some atonement that the hero must make with a father figure and a realization that the thing that is being searched for has been with them the entire time, like Dorothy's ruby slippers that allowed her to go home whenever she wanted.

You see, that saying, "It's not about the destination; it's about the journey" is totally true. It's not about where you are going. It's about who you are becoming and what you are overcoming. A caterpillar could never make the incredible journey that a butterfly can. Even if it thought it was tough and brave, it's just not equipped to make that flight of sometimes 100 miles per day. 2 Corinthians 5:17 says, "If anyone is in Christ, (s)he is a new creation; old things have passed away; behold all things have become new."

Sometimes we don't know whether we are coming or going. But it doesn't really matter. It's all the same because the joy is in the journey. It's in the discovery - or rediscovery that you are a beautiful, wonderful child of God. When you step into the role and that identity, you become larger. When you realize the power and strength of God and that He can help in any circumstance, no problem is too massive or difficult to handle.

Reflection Questions for Journaling or Group Discussion

- What is something that you need to overcome? What currently prevents you from flying over that hurdle?

  ____

  ____

  ____

- What are you afraid of? What would you do if you weren't afraid?

  ____

  ____

  ____

- As the hero of your story, identify which "anti-action" things are keeping you the most stuck in moving forward in your journey.

  ____

  ____

  ____

CHAPTER Thirteen: A WONDER WOMAN IS POWERFUL

Never forget that the most powerful force on earth is love.
- Nelson Rockefeller

If power is available to us to overcome the challenges we face on this journey, how do we tap into it? Just like radio waves exist all around us, there is power everywhere. Until electricity was discovered, we had no understanding of this power. People have seen the effects of lightning since the beginning of mankind - but we had no way of utilizing it. Just take a moment to think about how life on this planet has been transformed by tapping into this source. It's truly mind boggling.

You are an amazing and wonderful masterpiece. But without the electrical impulses that keep your heart pumping blood through your veins and arteries, your body does no good and you die. If you think about any electrical device from a simple lamp to a supercomputer, it is useless without electricity. You need to plug in so that your light can shine, and you need to connect so that you can serve the purpose to which you were created. Even if you have a battery, that can only last you so long. You need to be consistently connected in order to re-charge.

Sometimes we think we can do it all without connecting to the Spirit. We go and go and do and do, but eventually we over-do it. Have you ever had a laptop overheat because you were using the battery too long? We have a human term for that - it's called burn-out. The only solution is to turn off and plug in. If you ignore this and keep working, your computer can heat up to the point where it turns off all by itself. When you later come back to your work, you may have to reset or refresh your settings.

My friend Amy Allgood is a beautiful wonder woman who created a women's retreat called "Refresh" because she saw how many women were getting burnt out by the fast pace of today's world. If you are feeling stuck and things just aren't working for you, one of the best things you can do is to get away from the normal every day to re-connect with God, es-pecially in nature. Being in creation has a wonderful way of grounding you to the source of the power that sustains you. It also gives you a tremendous perspective. When you look at the ocean or the stars in the sky, you can't help but realize the vastness of the universe. Problems that seemed so large one moment now look miniscule in comparison.

In today's world, we not only rely on electricity, but also on the power of the internet and Wi-Fi. Although your device may still be on, if your device cannot connect, it can't function in the same way you want it to. When you finally do connect, you usually have to "refresh" your page so that it can work again. Taking a *break* from routine allows you to figuratively 'flip the breakers' if we are keeping the electrical/ computer analogy going.

Obviously, traveling to some remote destination or taking time away can be hard to do when you have so many responsibilities. If you can find a way to even take just a little time for yourself, it will be worth it for everyone. You can't keep going on an empty gas tank. So many women run themselves ragged until they are left running on fumes.

Psalm 23 is a famous passage of Scripture that I think everyone should memorize. If you don't know it, it says (NIV): "The Lord is my shepherd. I lack nothing. He makes me lie down in green pastures. He leads me beside quiet waters, he refreshes my soul." I'm going to pause here to point out that when we connect to the Spirit, we allow ourselves to be put in His care and protection. We don't need to worry what wolves are out there because He is good and stays by our side if we stay by His. He gives us abundance and we lack nothing. And notice that our souls are refreshed by quiet waters. There is something about the sound of water that calms and restores us. If you go on YouTube or buy a sound machine to help you sleep at night, although you can find some soundtracks with horns and sirens for those who are used to living in the city, most of the time you usually find the sound of a babbling brook or ocean waves. Water cleanses not only our bodies but our minds and souls as well. (On a side note, this is the symbolism of baptism in water. Depending on what tradition you come from, baptism is also accompanied by the giving of a name. A name is your identity, so when you receive a new name, it helps you step in the new creation of your being).

Going back to Psalm 23, it later says, "You anoint my head with oil, my cup overflows." When we are in God's presence, our cup is filled up. What we give to others should come from the overflow of our hearts. I've seen so many women (mothers in particular) who feel like they have nothing more to give. They may give because they feel they must, but their service to their families is no longer done with a joyful heart. If you are feeling this way, you need to find the courage to ask for help or at least help from your family to understand you will be a better person if you take some time to care for yourself. Even if it's just a bath with some of that fake babbling brook meditative music, it will help you to relax, refocus, and reconnect with your spiritual strength. Taking time to care for yourself is necessary, just like stopping to pull over and refuel your car is not selfish. Yes, it may take time to pull over and refuel, but obviously it is a much better alternative than being stuck on the side of the road for hours waiting for someone to help. You can either pause now or pause later. Pausing later will not get you to your destination in a timely manner and your journey will be much less pleasant.

In life there are many things where we either pay now or pay later. It may seem tempting to pay later, but there are usually hidden costs to this, (analogous to interest on your credit card). The longer you wait to pay, the more you will end up paying. You can pay for a gym membership now or diet solutions later. If you wait too long, you may even be paying for diabetes treatments or the like for the rest of your life. You can pay for marriage counseling now or divorce attorneys later. It may not be a physical payment of money, but it is often a "payment" of time and attention as well.

There's a famous concept and book called, *How Full is Your Bucket?*[29] by Tom Rath and Donald Clifton. The theory is that every interaction that we have is either a bucket-filling experience or a bucket-dipping experience. Some interactions leave you fuller and others leave you feeling drained. There are some people you meet who just constantly drain buckets and others who constantly fill others because they are overflowing. As a wonder woman, be that overflowing bucket, but also learn to say no to people who take too much of your energy.

Take time from each day to invest in your connection to the Spirit. Refill your cup by meditating, journaling, going on a walk in nature by yourself, reading the Bible or other inspirational books, painting, or whatever fills you up the most. If you feel like you don't have time to do those things, there are probably things that you are doing that you shouldn't. We all have 24 hours in a day. Look at what is on your "proverbial plate." Think of it like a pie chart and see how it is divided up. If you do this every day of the week for one week straight you will see patterns emerging that you perhaps didn't know were there. You'll soon see the things that have become idols in your life when you see how much time is being spent on those things. The things we spend our money and time on are the things we value most.

An often-quoted illustration regarding priorities is the "big rock" story, which was first popularized in Stephen Covey's book, *First Things First.*[30] A professor once stood in front of a classroom and put a large jar in front of his students. He then started filling the jar with some large rocks until he had about a dozen inside. He then asked the students if the jar was full, to which they all agreed that it was. He then reached behind the desk and pulled out a bucket of small stones and started pouring them into the jar, which slid down among the larger rocks. He then asked the students again if the jar was full. They were starting to catch on and answered that it probably was not. He smiled and reached down for a bucket of sand and started dumping the sand down into the spaces that were still left and asked again if the jar was full. It looked very full, but the students were unsure at this point. The professor then brought out a pitcher of water and began to pour it in until it was filled to the brim. The point of the illustration, he said, was that if you don't put your big rocks in first, you'll never get them in at all. He says, "What are the big rocks in your life? A project that you want to accomplish? Time with your loved ones? Your faith, your education, your finances? A cause? Teaching or mentoring others? Remember to put these 'Big Rocks' in first or you'll never get them in at all."

While this is a great analogy, life also doesn't work exactly this way. We can't just pour the little things in at the end of our lives. In reality, we have to have balance... big rock, then sand, then water. You can't completely ignore the sink disposal if you have a leak, or it will become a huge problem. You can't ignore taking time to pay your bills, or your big rocks will suffer. The point is though that you must have priorities in life and realize that you can not possibly fit everything that you want, so you must choose wisely. In today's world, there are many things that we can do to automate the little things, so that we can take the time to take care of the big things. By setting up automatic payments for your bills, trying a meal prep or delivery service, setting up regular maintenance for your home etc., you save yourself time doing the small things, so that you can focus on your bigger goals.

In physics, power is defined by the equation: *work divided by time*. The more work that can be done in a smaller amount of time, the more powerful something is. The definition of work in physics terms is force times displacement. Think of an excavator digging dirt. It is much more powerful than a human with a shovel because it can dig (or displace) a larger amount of dirt in a shorter amount of time. The term velocity means the speed of something in a given direction and can be written as displacement divided by time - like how far a car can go (miles per hour). So, power can also be defined as force times velocity. The horsepower of a car literally referred to the number of horses it would have taken to do the same job. Power increases your capabilities (maybe that's why so many superheroes wear capes… get it cape- abilities??) Ok. Sorry for the corny humor.

When we have power, we can expand our growth exponentially. In math, an exponent is literally called a power. If we really want to become more and expand into our potential, we need to get into a position that both enables us to receive that power and to do something amazing with it. A seed has the potential to become a massive sequoia if it has the blueprints for that in its DNA. If that seed sits on the shelf, it can never do that though. It needs to be planted where it receives energy from the earth, water, and sun to become what it was created to be. You must position yourself in such a way as to receive power and then release power.

You are an instrument to bring the light of the Spirit into the world. If you are plugged in, but not turned on and working, you also don't serve your mission. Ephesians 2:10 says, "We are His workmanship, created in Christ Jesus for good works." Sometimes we think we are too small or too weak to accomplish the things that Spirit has given us to do. Fortunately, the Bible shows us a well-run track record of weak people being made strong and mighty through the power of the Spirit. Almost all our Biblical "heroes" were just ordinary, fumbling, and broken people. 2 Corinthians 12:9 says, "My grace is sufficient for you, for my power is made perfect in weakness."

The Japanese art of kintsugi is a beautiful thing to behold and a wonderful metaphor for our lives. If a piece of pottery is broken, instead of throwing it away, they will repair it with gold. The gold still shows where the brokenness occurred, but your focus is on the entire beauty of the wholeness of the piece. Instead of being an ordinary piece of dinnerware, that plate or cup is transformed into a work of art. I discovered this metaphor when I was personally very broken from some things that occurred in my life. When you feel so weak and broken that you don't know how to put the pieces back together, ask the Spirit to mend you with gold.

God wants you to be strong so that you can do wonder-full things in this world. I think we often must realize our own brokenness and fragility though, so that we realize the gift that we have been given. It is by God's grace that we receive power. Now that it is clear that our power comes from the Holy Spirit and we know how to receive that power, let's get stronger.

Reflection Questions for Journaling or Group Discussion

- In what ways can you make time to recharge and reset so that you can live in the full power of your potential?

  ____

  ____

  ____

- How full is your bucket? Are you pouring out stress and frustration or are you overflowing with joy and love? Make a list of 5 or 6 of your top priorities or "big rocks." Are you making time to fit these into your life?

  ____

  ____

  ____

- How is God's power made perfect in our weakness? In what areas do you need to let God repair you with gold?

  ____

  ____

  ____

CHAPTER *Fourteen:* A WONDER WOMAN IS STRONG

Do you not know? Have you not heard? The LORD is the everlasting God, the Creator of the ends of the earth. He will not grow tired or weary, and his understanding no one can fathom. He gives strength to the weary and increases the power of the weak. Even youths grow tired and weary, and young men stumble and fall; but those who hope in the LORD will renew their strength. They will soar on wings like eagles; they will run and not grow weary, they will walk and not be faint. Isaiah 40:28-31

When we think of being strong, there are many images that may come to mind. We may think of things that are mighty and have a presence, like a lion or a bodybuilder. It's interesting though, that small things can also be very strong. The other day, my daughter found a scarab beetle in our backyard. I know the ancient Egyptians often used the scarab beetle in their drawings and writings as a symbol of transformation, resurrection, and strength. Scarab beetles can carry 1,000 times their own weight. Meanwhile, the strongest human bodybuilder can lift at a maximum around four times their own weight. Obviously, the larger the animal, the greater the overall power it has, so there is something to be said for size. But I want to take a moment for us to think about how powerful things can come in small packages as well and how we as women can increase our strength. Generally, women are smaller than our male counterparts, and we have often been referred to as the "weaker sex." Because of our size in a male-dominated world, we have had to overcome incredible odds and downright persecution to be where we are today as women. While there are still many cultures around the world where women are not free, women have been able to now prove that we can compete with men and even excel past them in education. There are now many more women getting higher education degrees than men. We live longer, have a higher tolerance for pain, and in general are much stronger than we have been given credit for.

On an interesting side note, it has been shown in nature that when the pressure is on with regard to the environment or famine, many more females are born than males. The male embryo does not withstand the pressure and is more likely to die, thereby favoring an increase in female births. Where I live in Florida, we can witness sea turtle nesting, and my children and I often go out on the beach at sunrise to see baby sea turtles making their way to the ocean (a wonder-full experience, I might add). I was recently made aware that sea turtle gender is affected by the heat of the sand in which the eggs were laid. When the sand gets hot, the more likely it is that the turtle will become female. With global warming and other environmental factors, a greater majority of turtles are becoming female. While we obviously need male and female for the species to survive, it's interesting to note how females can take the heat. When the pressure is on, women excel and show our hidden strength. Why do we keep our strength so hidden though? I believe a woman's strength is her secret weapon.

In the Biblical story of David and Goliath, David was a small shepherd boy, and Goliath was a giant man almost ten feet tall. No one could defeat this man in battle, but David did by using a small stone that hit him in the forehead, killing him instantly. David was strong because he knew the power of God and had confidence in that power. While others looked at him as being weak, he knew he had a secret weapon.

The thing about David was that this wasn't the first time he faced a formidable opponent. Before he faced Goliath, he had wrestled with a lion and a bear who were trying to steal his sheep. He was strong because he had faced trials and overcome them. Strength comes from repeated persistence against resistance. When you lift weights, it makes you stronger because you are giving your muscles a little more than you think you can handle or at least more than you would normally carry. That undertaking literally breaks apart or makes tiny tears in your muscles, which can then be built up larger than before.

If you look at your past, no matter who you are, the battles you've faced and overcome and the things that try to break you down, make you stronger in the long run. As Friedrich Nietzsche (and various musicians since then) has said, "What does not kill me makes me stronger." While we all want to have a safe, easy life, this path does not set us toward growth and strength – and the safe path is also not that exciting. In any good book or movie, there is always a major challenge to be faced at the climax. The protagonist needs to overcome to emerge as the hero.

It's interesting, but we need these challenges to be able to grow strong. Scientists made a very surprising discovery when they created the Biosphere 2, which is a man-made facility that has been created to mimic many of earth's ecological systems. When the trees were first planted, they were growing faster than they would have in nature. Before they could mature, however, they would collapse and fall over. The scientists had forgotten to include a key element in the design: wind. In the wild, wind gives a tree natural resistance as it grows, and therefore, its roots grow deeper, and its girth is wider to accommodate this. This is an important lesson for us, and, if we raise children, not to make the path too easy for them.

While in a previous chapter, we talked about resistance as being something to release, it is also something we need to propel us toward achieving our goals and greater freedom for ourselves and others. Think of a spring on a trampoline or any other spring you can think of. You need pressure on that spring for it to create tension until it is eventually released, and it propels you into the air. Obviously, a trampoline is not a great example because you don't keep going in one direction toward a goal, but in other ways it's a wonder-full example because it shows how you can still have fun while becoming strong. Any kind of strength training involves repeated motions because it is the back and forth pushing against the resistance and release of resistance that works the muscles. Newton's third law of motion says, "for every action, there is an equal and opposite reaction." If a bodybuilder wants to bench press a certain amount of weight, they actually have to build up the muscles that would react to that weight. That means doing squats and building up the leg muscles. They must squat down in order to lift up. In the arm, although we often think of our bicep muscles, it's really our posterior triceps muscles that are the largest and most utilized in doing overhead lifting.

So, what is the opposite and equal reaction to the battles and trials we might face? It's something you might not expect: our wonder-full secret strength is our joy! Nehemiah 8:10 says, "The joy of the Lord is our strength." Joy is such a powerful weapon because it diffuses any attack that can come against us. If someone comes at us with angry or accusing words, we can choose to look at them with compassion and non-judgement. We can realize that someone else's negativity does not necessarily have to influence our state of being. We have greater control and strength when we can choose our attitudes and choose to remain free of the funk that is going on around us. In this way, joy is a shield for us. Any fiery darts are put out by the fountain of joy inside us. Joy is also a weapon against darkness because it acts like a beacon of light, and it draws people toward you that have been held captive by the darkness. Of course, it's easy to be happy when everything is going well. True joy is revealed, however, when you can be happy even amid trials. If your light shines during the day, it may not be noticeable, but if it shines through the darkness, that light will be evident.

James 1:2-4 says that we should actually be thankful for our trials: "Consider it pure joy when you encounter trials of many kinds, because you know that the testing of your faith develops perseverance. Allow perseverance to finish its work, so that you may be mature and complete, not lacking anything." You might be wondering if James was high or something when he wrote this. Why would we want to consider it a joy to face a trial? Because it means you are ready for the test to advance to the next level in your growth. When we persevere, we can then become mature and complete. We need to *pass through the storm in order to transform.*

The reason a scarab beetle is also considered strong is because of its high level of persistence. We become what we continually do. If one person worked out six hours a day for a week straight and then never again for the rest of the year and another person worked out for seven minutes each day for the entire year, who do you think would be stronger at the end of the year? My bet is on the 7 minutes per day. It is about the same amount of time, but it's amazing what a small amount over a consistent period can look like. I really started improving in my fitness journey when I gave up my fancy gym membership and started doing a free 7-minute app by Johnson and Johnson. The key is consistency. There is a book by Jaroldeen Edwards called *The Daffodil Principle.*[31] It tells the story of one woman who, by planting daffodils daily over the course of twenty-five years, created an amazing five-acre field of 50,000 bulbs. It is the *sequence* of the habits we have that create the *con-sequences* of our lives.

It is the *routines* of our lives that create the *route* or path that our lives will go in. Kierkegaard once said, "Our life always expresses the result of our dominant thoughts," and modern psychology has shown this to be true as they study our neural networks and how we can re-wire our brains and our lives by changing our thought patterns. There's a reason a locomotive is also called a train. It goes repetitively over and over the same tracks. In the next chapter, we will be diving more into this *train*-ing.

Reflection Questions for Journaling or Group Discussion

- List some of the trials you have faced. In what ways have they made you stronger?

- How can you look at the trials you have faced or may be facing with joy? If you were to view your tests as a way of advancing to the next level, how would it change your perspective?

- What do you think are your strengths? If you are unsure, a helpful online assessment can be found at https://www.gallup.com/cliftonstrengths/en/254033/strengthsfinder.aspx

CHAPTER *Fifteen:* A WONDER WOMAN TRAINS

"Do you not know that in a race all the runners run, but only one gets the prize? Run in such a way as to get the prize. Everyone who competes in the games goes into strict training. They do it to get a crown that will not last, but we do it to get a crown that will last forever."
– 1 Corinthians 9: 24-25

If we are going to be strong in our joy, we need to get into the habit of creating joy in our life. As I write this, I am currently doing something called the 40-day joy challenge (joychallenge.com). This challenge helps you to be intentional about strengthening your joy muscles. Another great challenge is the the "love dare," which inspires you over the course of 40 days to love your spouse in various ways.[32] I recommend both because just like we train our physical body, we need to train our spiritual body. 1 Timothy 4:7,8 says, "Train yourself to be godly. For physical training is of some value, but godliness has value for all things, holding promises for both the present life and the life to come." When I started these challenges, I thought I was a fairly joyful and loving person. I've always tried to be optimistic, and I've had people say that I'm the most joyful person they know. But doing this training has made me realize how often I can still be negative, unloving, and unappreciative. It's like when you do a workout that addresses muscles you don't always exercise. Although I've gotten into jogging and feel relatively fit, a friend of mine has been doing these HIT (high interval training) workouts at 5:45am and invites me to do them with her via Zoom three days a week. Thank goodness for friends who motivate us! They are just free videos on YouTube, but oh believe me.... I now feel muscles I didn't know were there.

It's interesting how the term "work out" came into our nomenclature. It's a relatively recent term (only used in the last 100 years or so) and was originally a boxing term. In earlier times if you had a dispute with someone, you could go into a boxing ring and "work out" your differences. I'm not sure if that's literally how the term came about, but it's a good visual example of how we need to wrestle with many things until they no longer exist. When you work out a problem, that means you re-solve or dissolve it until it disappears. Think not of two people in a ring, but you against whatever issue has control over you. As we work out against the strongholds in our lives, we can hopefully become stronger with the Spirit's power and defeat those things until they are knocked out.

Strongholds in your life are anything that exists that prevents you from living in the freedom that the Spirit offered us through the saving work Christ accomplished for us on the cross. We have been offered the chance to be saved from slavery, and yet we somehow can't believe this great gift sometimes and therefore still sit in our chains. Philippians 2: 12-13 tells us to "continue to *work out* your salvation with fear and trembling. For it is God who works in you to will and to act on behalf of His good purposes." These verses do not mean we need to work *for* our salvation. The Spirit has done that for us. Verses 1-11 that are written previous to this says,

"Therefore, if you have any encouragement from being united with Christ, if any comfort from his love, if any common sharing in the Spirit, if any tenderness and compassion, then make my joy complete by being like-minded, having the same love, being one in spirit and of one mind. Do nothing out of selfish ambition or vain conceit. Rather, in humility value others above yourselves, not looking to your own interests but each of you to the interests of the others. In your relationships with one another, have the same mindset as Christ Jesus: Who, being in very nature God, did not consider equality with God something to be used to his own advantage; rather, he made himself nothing by taking the very nature of a servant, being made in human likeness. And being found in appearance as a man, he humbled himself by becoming obedient to death— even death on a cross! Therefore God exalted him to the highest place and gave him the name that is above every name, that at the name of Jesus every knee should bow, in heaven and on earth and under the earth, and every tongue acknowledge that Jesus Christ is Lord, to the glory of God the Father."

Going back to the butterfly example, this "working out" is more like what the caterpillar undergoes in metamorphosis. It dissolves itself into nothing so that it can then be rearranged into something new. It literally works its way out of its cocoon into the freedom of its new state. As we work out the body and the mind, we help bring it into submission. When we deny ourselves junk foods or fast from things, we are aligning ourselves into a place of humility where we can allow God's power to flow. We can be so much stronger when we allow the power of God to flow and strengthen us. When we are proud of our own strength, it acts like a barrier to God's power. 1 Peter 5:5-6 says that "God opposes the proud but shows favor to the humble. Humble yourselves, therefore, under God's mighty hand, that He may lift you up in due time. Peter is quoting Proverbs 3:34, which says that the Lord mocks proud mockers but is gracious to the humble. (Proverbs 3 is a wonder-full chapter by the way if you want to take a moment to go and read it).

As humans, we don't like to be humble. We like to be acknowledged, praised, and liked. In today's world, in particular, our whole social media platforms are built upon the idea that we are all looking for validation. When we have a lot of "likes" on our social media feeds, we feel good, but if we put too much emphasis on this, it can also make us feel bad about ourselves when we don't have many "likes" or when we start on the dangerous road of social media comparison.

I feel like humility is a trait that is very rare to find in today's society. It's not really something that we even value as a quality to be desired. Pride, however, or a lack of humility, is really the source of almost all the sins we struggle with. Whatever we're facing, our pride is at the heart of it and shows us our heart. Even after I was writing these verses on humility, I found myself one day grumbling to myself about how much laundry I had to do or picking up puppy poop from our carpet. And do you know who this kind of thinking was hurting? Me! It was my joy that was being compromised. Instead of being thankful for the children I had longed and prayed for, I was grumbling about how much laundry they make. Instead of being thankful for a puppy that I had wanted to have ever since I was a child, I was grumbling and thinking there must be something better. Fortunately, I was able to be aware of these thoughts and extinguish them because I've been training my mind to be strong and to detect these enemy influences. Instead, I started to think of things to be grateful for - for the quiet time to pray or listen to audio teachings, for the fact that I have the financial freedom to be home with my children right now, for carpets that resist pet stains, for a working washer and dryer etc. You see, gratitude and humility go hand in hand. In the past, I could have allowed those things to rob me and my family of joy.

I know you may be thinking that it is ironic that the last chapter talked about being a strong wonder woman, and now we are now talking about humility. I hope that you have been able to see, however, that *true strength is found in humility*. It doesn't matter how successful or how many muscles you can show off if you are cocky or a brag. Not only are other people not attracted to these qualities, but as Thomas Merton once said, "Pride makes us artificial, and humility makes us real." Being humble is being true to yourself and true to others so that you can truly be free and set others free. A macho muscle man who lifts weights all day may be strong, but if he doesn't do anything to help lift others up, what good is that strength?

A great little story that illustrates how pride can bring us down is *Gertrude McFuzz*[33] by the legendary Dr. Seuss. In this tale, a bird named Gertrude wants to have more feathers so that she can be prettier than "Lolla-Lee-Lou." She is told to eat the pill berry bush to get more feathers, which does work. But instead of just eating a few, she eats the whole bush. Soon, she has so many feathers that she can't even fly (not a good place to be for a bird). What a great visual example of what pride can do to us. It may look pretty from the outside, but it drags us down. We all know the expression, "pride comes before a fall," which is really shortened from Proverbs 16:18, which says, "Pride goes before destruction, a haughty spirit before a fall."

Now, you might be asking yourself though, well, "shouldn't we have pride in our work?" My answer would be no. I think that term is too overused and probably the reason we have so many workaholics in our culture. We need to have joy in our work, contentment in our work, delight, gratification, fulfillment, satisfaction - there are many other words used to describe how we can enjoy what we do and do a job well done. I love this quote by C.S. Lewis: "Humility is not thinking less of yourself, it's thinking of yourself less." You don't have to have poor self-esteem or a poor work ethic to be humble. Christ told us in Matthew 20:26-28, "Whoever wants to become great among you must be your servant, and whoever wants to be first must be your slave — just as the Son of Man did not come to be served, but to serve, and to give his life as a ransom for many." He also says in Matthew 23:11-12 that, "The greatest among you will be your servant. For those who exalt themselves will be humbled, and those who humble themselves will be exalted." Christ was the ultimate example for us of strength and humility. He washed his disciples' feet. How much more should we serve one another?

Paul says in 2 Corinthians 12, if you are going to boast about anything, boast about your weaknesses, so as the "weaker sex," we are already in a position to allow God's strength to show through us. He says in verses 9 and 10, "Therefore I will boast all the more gladly about my weaknesses, so that Christ's power may rest on me. That is why, for Christ's sake, I delight in weaknesses, in insults, in hardships, in persecutions, in difficulties. For when I am weak, then I am strong." In the next chapter, we will discover how we can develop our strength to be a warrior who can battle through these trials and to be the hero you were made to be.

Reflection Questions for Journaling or Group Discussion

- What strongholds are keeping you bound?

____

____

____

- How can you work out your salvation so that you are truly living in a state of freedom and joy? Make a date with yourself to take on the Love Dare or the 40 day Joy Challenge.

____

____

____

- How can humility be the ultimate show of strength? How can you train yourself to live more in humility when the world around us values pride?

____

____

____

CHAPTER *Sixteen:* A WONDER WOMAN IS A WARRIOR

> *"You are braver than you believe, stronger than you seem, and smarter than you think. But the most important thing is, even if we're apart... I'll always be with you."*
> *– Winnie the Pooh*

We need to realize that we are made strong for a purpose - and that is not only for ourselves to be free but also to free others and to lift them up. It takes a lot more physical strength to lift someone up than to push them down - and the same is true in the spiritual sense.

The term warrior has the word "war" in it for a reason. You cannot be a *warrior* without having to go to *war*. While no one likes war, like we looked at previously, we sometimes need to fight battles to free others or even ourselves. A wonder woman has power, not just so that she can show off.... she has power so that she can fight against those who bring destruction and have selfish motives.

Ephesians 6:10 says, "Be strong in the Lord and in the strength of his might. Put on the whole armor of God, that you may stand against the schemes of the devil. For we do not wrestle against flesh and blood, but against the rulers, against authorities, against the cosmic powers over this present darkness, against the spiritual forces of evil in the heavenly places."

In the following chapters, we will explore this armor more specifically, but I want to stop first to talk about the invisible battle. It seems like science fiction to talk about invisible battles. I personally have never liked to acknowledge the fact that there might be invisible forces out there, but I do want to take this time to explore the possibility. Just like we can't see sound waves or electricity or even many invisible waves of light, there are other dimensions that we cannot perceive with our senses. In string theory, scientists propose that there may be ten to eleven dimensions that exist. Our minds can't even conceive of what this means. If you are interested, a good primer on these ideas is called *The Elegant Universe.*[34] I've been fascinated by string theory because I feel that it ties science and spirit together. For thousands of years, spiritual teachers have been speaking about vibrations and energy, and science is also now unraveling these mysteries in a mathematical way. The uni-verse is basically one verse of a song. There may even be multiple verses of this song (the mulit-verse). What we perceive and don't perceive results from the harmony or discord of the various players and instruments.

How does this all relate back to being a strong warrior? As Paulo Coelho, author of the amazing tale, *The Alchemist,*[35] puts it, we are called to be *Warriors of the Light.* Only 5% of the universe consists of visible matter and energy. The other 95% consists of what scientists deem dark energy and dark matter. Now, I'm not equating dark matter and energy with spiritual forces of darkness. These are simply particles of energy and are necessary for our universe to exist. What I want to convey is an analogy to dark and light energy with regards to being a warrior. The light energy must overcome a lot to be seen. As the 5% minority, its force must be strong to do its job.

Light is so powerful when it is present because whatever and wherever it touches, darkness cannot exist. Things that seem so scary and unknown in the dark are seen as mere shadows and illusions when the lights are turned on. It's interesting that so many of the crimes and evil things that happen in this world take place after the sun sets. It makes you wonder if evil spirits are literally energized by the darkness and weakened by the light.

It's interesting too, how we refer to hard alcohol as "spirits" and much of the consumption of these spirits takes place after dark. What if, by taking in these spirits into our bodies – which are supposed to be the temples of the Holy Spirit – we are instead inviting other spirits to dwell inside us? I have seen firsthand the destructive nature of alcohol in my own family. While a "little wine is good for the stomach" (1 Timothy 5:23) and Jesus's first miracle was turning water into wine, we just have to be careful with how much we consume. We know that alcohol depresses our senses and makes us feel good, but it also makes us less alert and more susceptible to all kinds of influences.

If we were in a war, what a great strategy it would be for the enemy to use. Instead of having to fight, they could just slip someone over the border with the entertaining spirits of alcohol. Picture in your mind an army troop intoxicated and jovial one night, while the enemy is surrounding them, ready to attack them after they are too sloppy to fight. While alcohol or any drug can make you feel happy or even euphoric, it is not a true joy, and the hangover you experience afterward is the result of this illusion. True joy never has negative results because joy recognizes those hard things as learning and growth experiences.

There are things about the spirit realm we may not understand because these things (at least with our current technology) cannot be tested with our scientific instruments. Less than 200 years ago, we did not have the instruments to detect radio waves. That does not mean these waves did not exist prior to this; we just could not detect or understand them. We are spiritual beings having a human experience, but we have no idea how we do this. We incarnate into these bodies and when our bodies have completed their life cycle, we depart to another spiritual realm. If you can acknowledge however that we are spirits, then it makes sense to also believe that some of us occasionally get lost and can't find our way. If a spirit acts selfishly or loses their path while on this human journey, perhaps they get demoted and become de-men? The spirits then go around trying to oppress or possess susceptible humans who have perhaps opened a door to them through some means like alcohol.

This is obviously just a thought theory and I have no proof of this, but we do need to think and be aware that there may be invisible forces that we just don't understand. Like the wind is invisible, we can see its effects as either a nice breeze that cools us or a destructive hurricane or tornado that destroys everything in its path. We don't think about the wind around us until it's gathered in a strong force. When it does start to gather, we track it and prepare for the onslaught. As I write this, we've lived in Florida for four years and we've had major hurricanes head our way every year since we've been here. Each time we've been spared, but we still prepare to evacuate if necessary.

If we are to be warriors of the light, we need to prepare ourselves with the right tools and the right strategy. There's an old expression that says, "don't use a cannon to kill a mosquito." We have to know our enemy and use the right equipment. As you can imagine, we get quite a few mosquitoes in Florida as well. Sometimes they make their way into the house. When I get up in the morning, I sometimes like the light low, but if there is a mosquito in the room, I need to turn those lights on brightly in order to see my "enemy." I know it's there... I can hear it, but it's the mosquito's blood or mine, and if I don't turn the light on, I will pay the itchy consequences later. If it were only an itchy bump, it wouldn't be that serious, but mosquitoes also carry viruses and parasites that cause many deadly diseases. In some parts of the world, that mosquito bite could mean the literal difference between life and death. When my sister was traveling in southeast Asia, they used mosquito zappers that look like tennis rackets to kill these pests, and I thought it was such a great idea that I purchased a few to have around our home as well. While we also have the kind of zapper that passively will kill a mosquito that gets too close, our racket zappers are the right tool to get the job done.

When I studied public "health," most of our focus actually ended up being on diseases. We must know the enemy in order to defeat it. By understanding the biology and life cycle of both the mosquito and the parasite that causes malaria, preventative measures can be taken, as well as medications that treat the disease. I'm not saying we need to be obsessed with learning about evil or that we should blame every bad thing we do or that others do on invisible evil forces. That can be a bad path to follow because it can sometimes lead us away from the Light. Many ideas and depictions of evil come from ancient or pagan religions, so we need to be careful about what we believe. The Spirit knows all things and I believe he knows that we need both the dark and the light in our lives; it is not inherently "evil." Without the darkness, we would never be able to see the beauty of the stars at night. Without the darkness, we would not be able to sleep as well and dream. It is in the darkness that we realize the need for the light and seek it out. Like Job being allowed to be tested by Satan, the darkness allows us to really see how bright our light really is.

But when you see the sun rising and know that it is the day, you wake up from that dream to reality and realize the things that you thought were real were just an illusion. Some people have trained themselves to then go back into their dreams at night in a more awakened state - where they realize that they are dreaming. This is called lucid dreaming. When you are aware that you are dreaming, you can alter the dream because you know that it is just an illusion. This has happened to me just a few times, and I should probably train myself to do it again because it is truly wonder-full. You can fly if you so choose and can really feel like a superhero. You can be a warrior and fight off any nightmares if you are able to stay in that awareness because you know that those things have no real power. Our "reality" is much like that dream state. Much of what we think we know is an illusion. There is much more than meets the eye. There are wars around us that we do not see.

When I was in junior high school, I did a science project on the immune system called "The Wars Within." Although we cannot see viruses and bacteria, they are there. Although people did not know this for thousands of years, we now believe this as a general population because we can see them through powerful microscopes. When a pathogen enters the body, we have cells that detect these invaders, and they sound the alarm for cells of the immune system to wage war against these attacks. That is one of the many reasons why it is so important to eat a healthy diet. The food that was given to us by God contains vitamins, minerals, proteins, and other useful artillery needed to create good defenses. Imagine an army without any weapons. What is worse is when we eat foods that intentionally bring cancer-causing free radicals into our bodies. We may see these foods as harmless, but if our immune systems are too tired from fighting these free radicals, it won't be able to fight off viral attacks. I like to think of free radicals in my mind as rogue terrorists that we are intentionally sneaking into our country. We wouldn't do this on purpose in real life, but we bring these carcinogens into our temples when we consume processed foods and meats, alcohol, genetically modified foods, soda, refined sugars and flour, conventional "dirty" fruits and vegetables sprayed with pesticides, and meats that have been exposed to hormones and toxins either intentionally or unintentionally.

In the same way, we can unintentionally yet intentionally, bring rogue terrorist spirits into our lives and homes by the things we watch and hear, and the thoughts we think. Just like the wars within our bodies on a micro scale, there are wars without on a macro scale that we could not see. My very first science project was on the solar system (can you tell I've always been on the nerdy side?). When we look up into the night sky, the stars seem so small because they are so far away. Little do we realize that many of those stars are larger than our own sun and little do we realize that our sun is so massive because even that closest star is 93 million miles away. Our family recently took a trip to Kennedy Space Center, and we'll leave it to say that we have all been space obsessed since that time. Even our four-year-old knows all the names of the planets and dwarf planets. When I did that science project, we did not even know that these dwarf planets existed. Can you even fathom how much more we have to learn about space? When the Hubble telescope is pointed at the darkest part of the sky where we thought no stars existed, they find not only are there stars, but that there are many galaxies, each filled with billions of stars. While it might seem like a tangent to talk about the micro and macro things we can't see, I'm trying to help us really have it sink in that just because we can't see something doesn't mean it doesn't exist.

So often we think our battles are with people: our spouses, children, coworkers, people of an opposite political party, or religious, economic, or ethnic group. In 1 Corinthians 12, the apostle Paul likens people to parts of one body:

12 Just as a body, though one, has many parts, but all its many parts form one body, so it is with Christ. 13 For we were all baptized by[c] one Spirit so as to form one body—whether Jews or Gentiles, slave or free—and we were all given the one Spirit to drink. 14 Even so the body is not made up of one part but of many.

15 Now if the foot should say, "Because I am not a hand, I do not belong to the body," it would not for that reason stop being part of the body. 16 And if the ear should say, "Because I am not an eye, I do not belong to the body," it would not for that reason stop being part of the body. 17 If the whole body were an eye, where would the sense of hearing be? If the whole body were an ear, where would the sense of smell be? 18

But in fact God has placed the parts in the body, every one of them, just as he wanted them to be. 19 If they were all one part, where would the body be? 20 As it is, there are many parts, but one body.

21 The eye cannot say to the hand, "I don't need you!" And the head cannot say to the feet, "I don't need you!" 22 On the contrary, those parts of the body that seem to be weaker are indispensable, 23 and the parts that we think are less honorable we treat with special honor. And the parts that are unpresentable are treated with special modesty, 24 while our presentable parts need no special treatment. But God has put the body together, giving greater honor to the parts that lacked it, 25 so that there should be no division in the body, but that its parts should have equal concern for each other. 26 If one part suffers, every part suffers with it; if one part is honored, every part rejoices with it.

We're all God's children. He came to save the whole world- not just the people we like. He came to save our "enemies" too. That is why Christ put such an emphasis on us loving one another - even our enemies. We are all probably familiar with the passage of scripture that follows Corinthians 12. First Corinthians 13 is called the "love" chapter and is often read during weddings. After the honeymoon is over, though, how long does it take for us as women to turn into the stereotypical nagging wife when we see our husbands or children not doing their parts. We focus on them not loving us enough- when really our focus needs to be on our love for them.

There is a movie called *War Room*[36] that is a wonderful illustration of the type of warrior we need to become. In the movie, a woman learns to battle in prayer to save her marriage. Her closet is converted into her war room, named after a place which army captains talk about strategy in battle. She learns that "in order to stand up and fight the enemy, you need to get on your knees and pray." While this may seem counter to our worldly inclination, I'm sure you're seeing a pattern by now that seems to be a running theme in this book. Whatever enemy or trial you are facing, the God who is bigger than this incredibly vast universe is far more capable of handling these problems than you can on your own. In prayer, we humble ourselves and ask God to do what we cannot do on our own.

In the book of Esther, the story is told of the queen who saved the entire nation of Israel. She didn't do it using a sword. Her weapon was fasting and prayer. In Esther 4:16 her words are recorded as the following, "Go, gather together all the Jews that are present in Shushan, and fast ye for me, and neither eat nor drink three days, night or day: I also and my maidens will fast likewise; and so will I go in unto the king, which is not according to the law: and if I perish, I perish."

The position that is strongest is one of prayer and praise. In another example from the Bible, the Israelites were about to be attacked by neighboring tribes. The first thing that Jehoshaphat did was to pray, and the Lord spoke to them through his prophet. 2 Chronicles 20:17 says, "You will not have to fight this battle. Take up your positions; stand firm and see the deliverance the Lord will give you, Judah and Jerusalem. Do not be afraid; do not be discouraged. Go out to face them tomorrow, and the Lord will be with you." In verse 21, it tells us that "Jehoshaphat appointed men to sing to the Lord and to praise him for the splendor of his holiness as they went out at the head of the army, saying:

"Give thanks to the Lord, for his love endures forever." As they began to sing and praise, the Lord set ambushes against the men of Ammon and Moab and Mount Seir who were invading Judah, and they were defeated. The Ammonites and Moabites rose up against the men from Mount Seir to destroy and annihilate them. After they finished slaughtering the men

from Seir, they helped to destroy one another.... The fear of God came on all the surrounding kingdoms when they heard how the Lord had fought against the enemies of Israel. And the kingdom of Jehoshaphat was at peace, for his God had given him rest on every side.

How awesome is that? Their weapon was worship, and they praised their way into victory.

Reflection Questions for Journaling or Group Discussion

- What are some things that you believe in even though you can't see or understand them?

  ____
  ____
  ____

- If we do not wrestle with "flesh and blood," then why do we spend so much time thinking that people are the enemy? If there is someone in your life who you view as an enemy, if you can't love them, work on at least forgiving them.

  ____
  ____
  ____

- How can prayer and praise be our biggest weapon as a warrior?

  ____
  ____
  ____

CHAPTER *Seventeen*: A WONDER WOMAN CARRIES THE RIGHT WEAPONS

For though we live in the world, we do not wage war as the world does. The weapons we fight with are not the weapons of the world. On the contrary, they have divine power to demolish strongholds. We demolish arguments and every pretension that sets itself up against the knowledge of God, and we take captive every thought to make it obedient to Christ.
- 1 Corinthians 10: 3-5

When I recently watched the 2017 *Wonder Woman* movie,[37] I noticed some great illustrations that we can look to as a model to follow. I won't spoil the film, but when Wonder Woman comes into the regular human world, she's dressed like a warrior. She has a special sword that she believes can kill Aries, the god of war. She also has her shield, some kick-ass boots, her lasso of truth, and amazing arm bands that protect her from all kinds of attacks. We'll just leave it to say she didn't exactly fit into the style of 1940's England. They tried to get her to put on the "normal" dress and to put down her weapons. She tried it, but she couldn't fight with all those extra clothes weighing her down.

I think we've often forgotten our inner hero because we have hidden our armor in our attempt to fit in with everyone else. Of course, we don't stand out as anything special because that's what we've been trying to do - just fit into the mold that has been given to us. If you take a moment to look around you, we've often accepted these cookie cutter lives. So many of us live in houses that look exactly like our neighbors. I'm guessing that 90% of you moms reading this, if you have more than one child, you likely drive an SUV or minivan and often feel like your professional job is taxi service for your kid's sports games or other extracurricular activities. We dress in brands that will be looked upon as stylish or that hints to a certain level of financial status. But in doing this, we're just becoming clones - buying into the stereotype of whatever the world is trying to sell us.

But a hero is not one who blends in with the crowd. A hero is someone who acts differently and who thinks differently. I always loved Apple's "Think Different" campaign, which showed various heroes of science, politics, adventure etc. who thought differently and changed the direction of the world because of it. There's that famous bumper sticker, "well behaved women rarely make history." This is unfortunate, but also often true. I don't think, however, that we have to be badly behaved; we just need to have the courage to step out of the mold that has been imposed on us.

It's interesting to note the two usages of the word mold. One is to form something into a particular shape, often being used again and again. The other is a fungus that grows on dead things. When you open the fridge and find that some fruit or vegetable has been pushed to the back, hidden and forgotten, what do you usually find on it? Mold. It wasn't utilized for the purpose that it was created for and just sat there, wasting away until it eventually had to be thrown away.

None of us wants to waste our lives, but why do we so often get trapped "in the back of the fridge?" While it's important to put others before ourselves, we also don't need to get stuck in a place where we've lost our own unique identity. We need to say "enough is enough." We can't fight our battles when we're not wearing the proper gear, and that gear is the armor of God. In Ephesians 6:10-17, the apostle Paul uses the analogy of armor.

Finally, be strong in the Lord and in his mighty power. Put on the full armor of God, so that you can take your stand against the devil's schemes. For our struggle is not against flesh and blood, but against the rulers, against the authorities, against the powers of this dark world and against the spiritual forces of evil in the heavenly realms. Therefore put on the full armor of God, so that when the day of evil comes, you may be able to stand your ground, and after you have done everything, to stand. Stand firm then, with the belt of truth buckled around your waist, with the breastplate of righteousness in place, and with your feet fitted with the readiness that comes from the gospel of peace. In addition to all this, take up the shield of faith, with which you can extinguish all the flaming arrows of the evil one. Take the helmet of salvation and the sword of the Spirit, which is the word of God.

In Paul's day, people were well familiar with the kind of armor he was talking about. They lived in a time of Roman occupation, and the Roman soldiers were everywhere, even in times of peace. Today's soldiers obviously don't go walking around with swords and shields. It's interesting that even soldiers today wear camouflage. Camouflage is nature's defense mechanism for animals hiding from predators. In today's world, we're all hiding. We're all on the defensive. We're all just trying to blend in. We're living in such a way as to not rock the boat. But Christ calls us to step out of the boat. He calls us to a wild faith that says, *if you trust in me, I will protect you and keep you from sinking.*

In the 2017 movie, Wonder Woman wants to go to the front line because she knows that is where the battle is fought and where the war will be won. Paul tells us that the sword we need to carry is the Word of God. The type of sword that Paul refers to here in Greek is the word, *machaira.* As you can imagine, there were many types of swords in ancient times. This particular type was a small sword: one that can be hidden and taken out quickly. It's handy and quick. Paul uses this same word in Hebrews 4:12 where he says, "For the Word of God is living and active and sharper than any two-edged sword, and pierces as far as the division of soul and spirit, of both joints and marrow, and able to judge the thoughts and intentions of the heart."

Although Paul uses an analogy of the Word of God being our sword in both this passage and in Ephesians 6, the term used for the "Word of God" in Greek are two different words. In Hebrews 4, he uses the more common word, *logos.* which is the Greek word for discourse and most often refers to written Scripture. This written word is so important because it is the training manual or script of our lives. If I buy a new appliance, but fail to read the instruction manual, it may work okay, but I may be missing out on how to use various features and what to do if it breaks down. If an actor fails to read the script, they won't be able to play their role. *Script-ure* is your (ure) Script. It gives you the clues you need to discover your purpose. When you read history, you see *His* (God's) *Story* in every aspect of the world. Your purpose may not be exactly laid out in specific directions. It's never written in big bold letters something like, "Adrienne, write a book to help women achieve their potential," but it does help us know what path to follow in a general way. It is a sword that helps you see the intentions of your heart. If they are in line with Scripture, advance; if not you have to (quoting monopoly) "go directly to jail... do not pass go… do not collect $200).

There's a Bible devotional app that I use called YouVersion. I love that name because you understand as you read the Word, that it helps you be the *version of you* that you desire to be. We don't need to be cookie cutter versions of each other. You are be-you-tiful when you embrace or are full of being who you were meant to be. I think one of our most innate human desires is to be known and loved for who we are - and yet so many of us hide our true self from others. We cover ourselves with masks and we fail to live lives of authenticity. There's a saying, "when the earth's people are real, then it will heal." It's interesting how we all got accustomed to wearing literal masks in the coronavirus pandemic. There were times I passed by people I knew and didn't even recognize them at first because I couldn't see who they really were. None of us like wearing masks literally, so we should avoid them figuratively if we can. We need to live lives of authenticity.

Getting back to Ephesians 6 and Paul's description of armor, the Greek word that he uses for "Word of God" here is the word *rhema*. This word means more like the spoken word or utterance. In this context, Paul uses the 'word of God' as meaning when we hear from the Holy Spirit directly. In Greek grammar, *rhema* is a verb, not a noun. Of course, God can speak to us through the written word, but here Paul is saying that the sword is something you take up when you hear a specific action from your commander or if you are directly being attacked. As we read the written word and memorize it, we can hide it in our hearts and sharpen it, but what good is it if we sit on the sidelines and never use it? The *rhema* of God is when we listen and do the specific thing that He is calling us to do. It may look very different from a battle, and in fact, it should. You are a warrior of the light. This means when you feel the calling to share the love of Christ with someone, you don't shrink back as a coward. You go forward and let God's rhema speak through you. When you see the hurting, you don't shirk away and say it's not my problem - you fight injustice with justice and pain with healing. Each time we fight with light, the darkness begins to diminish. The darkness holds many people in bondage. This sword or knife is with us to cut those cords that bind them as slaves. This sword is never to go to the captive and then hold it at their throat, telling them they must believe a certain way. I love to support organizations like Cure International, World Vision etc. because of this: they aim to simply help people out of their poverty and their infirmities. They don't say, "you have to believe in Jesus to have this food or surgery." The people just see the light of Christ shining through them and desire to have that light as well.

We can't all be missionaries to third world countries, but we can do what God is speaking to our hearts where we are and with the resources we have. We can step out and do something even if it is hard or may seem ridiculous. When God calls you to the front lines, it may be on your knees interceding for others. It may be leading your family and guiding your children and training them up to be warriors too. Each one of us has a unique fingerprint, and each one of us has our own unique mark to make in this world. When you are quiet, the rhema of the Spirit will guide you in how to pick up your sword and leave that mark.

The other offensive item that Wonder Woman famously carries is her lasso of truth. This is obviously not one of the items mentioned in Ephesians 6, but I want to take a moment to look at this lasso. When you think of a lasso, what is the first thing that comes to mind? For me, it is the wild west or cattle herding. A lasso is used to bring in part of the herd that has perhaps strayed. Unlike a regular lasso, when she uses it around them, the captives are forced to tell the truth. Interestingly, while the creator of Wonder Woman, William Moulton Marston, stated that the lasso represented the charms of a woman, he also developed the test for systolic blood pressure, which was used in the creation of the lie detector.

Truth is such an important aspect of life and light and yet so hard sometimes to discover. Once we feel like we know the truth, it is very tempting to want to hit people over the head with it. Although we want to live true, authentic lives, as women, we also have the power of our charms to help lasso in others to know the truth. As the old saying goes, "You attract more flies with honey than with vinegar." Authenticity doesn't mean that if you are feeling grumpy you should stay there, or what's worse, make everyone else around you miserable. Authenticity means acknowledging the feelings that are surfacing and working on YOURSELF to change those things - not blaming others.

It's interesting to note how many Bible verses there are that talk about a nagging or quarrelsome woman. Proverbs 21:19 says, "it is better to live in the desert than with a quarrelsome and fretful woman." Proverbs 27:15 says, "A continual dripping on a rainy day and a quarrelsome wife are alike." Solomon, who was the writer of most of the book of Proverbs, brought on many of his troubles with women by marrying way too many of them, but we shall still take the point that knowing the truth and helping others to see that truth can happen in very different ways. For example, it may be true that your children and husband are not helping enough with things around the house. We can either use the lasso of truth to make them feel the pain of our nagging until they give in, or we can gently reign them in with love by establishing a system for chores. Wonder Woman uses her lasso of truth harshly on her enemies and uses her lasso at other times to rescue people. We need to remember that our families are not our enemies! Let's follow Christ's example in all things. He knew the truth about all things. He knew the sins people had committed but he did not use harsh words or actions with them unless they were the ones representing God's work (he did a few times show some anger at those who were making profits in the temple or the religious Pharisees, for example). For the most part, he uses his "lasso of truth" to draw crowds to him to hear a message of love, healing, and redemption.

Living a true, authentic life will draw people to you because people will "wonder" what is different about you, and it gives you an opportunity to spread the light. The questions at the end of each chapter are here to help you to take the time to discover who you truly are and the unique fingerprint that you have. When we ask the Spirit to guide, the truth will reveal itself. Don't we all want to know and live out our life's purpose? If you want to find out the Spirit's purpose for you, you need to first ask. It may or may not be what you want to hear, but you have to be willing to listen and find out the truth. In Christian circles, everyone loves to quote Jeremiah 29:11, "For I know the plans I have for you, declares the Lord, plans to prosper you and not to harm you, plans to give you a hope and a future." But what most people forget is that the people had just been told they would be staying in exile for 70 years! A false prosperity prophet was telling the people that it would only be two years (read Jeremiah chapter 28 and the rest of chapter 29). Verses 12 and 13 that follow this famous verse says, "Then you will call on me and come to pray to me and I will listen to you. You will seek me and find me when you seek me with all your heart."

The Spirit will give us true peace and prosperity when we first seek with all our heart. The path or plan that we might follow may not look exactly like the one we would have chosen, but we need to rest in the knowledge that the Spirit sees a much bigger picture than we can. Although God wants to fill our lives with true joy in Him, oftentimes His plan is focused on making us holy… not just happy. We need to learn to listen to the rhema of God and know the truth, even when it's hard. The truth will ultimately set us free.

Now that we have discussed the weapons of spiritual warfare, I now want to move onto something really important: fashion. Ok, I'm kind of being sarcastic here, but seriously, we need to learn what to wear if we are going to bring out the warrior hero inside of us. We need to learn to dress the part and make sure we are wearing protective gear for the battle as well.

Reflection Questions for Journaling or Group Discussion

- Have you gotten stuck in a particular mold that the world tries to put you in? How can you get un-stuck and live the unique calling that God has given to you?

____

____

____

- How can you allow Scripture to become Your Script for living the life of a hero? If you really viewed it like that, would you just pick it up every once in a awhile or would you read it every day?

____

____

____

- How does living a life of authenticity and wonder draw people to you?

____

____

____

CHAPTER *Eighteen:* A WONDER WOMAN DRESSES FOR SUCCESS

The LORD is my strength and my shield; my heart trusts in him, and he helps me. My heart leaps for joy, and with my song I praise him. – Psalm 28:7

We don't often think of what we wear as our defenses, but that is what they were originally designed for: as protection against the elements, whether they be the cold or the burning sun. Your clothes are designed to be a shield. Shields are essential to carry in battle because it doesn't matter how sharp your sword is if you can't ward off an attack of flaming arrows headed your way. Offensive and defensive strategy are inextricably linked, and you can't win the battle if you aren't dressed for success.

I played basketball in high school, and it was there I learned that it doesn't matter how good your shooting is if you don't guard the ball or rebound the ball when you miss. You're never going to win if you let the other team score more than you do. When you're on a team, you all wear the same uniform so that you know who to pass the ball to and who to keep it away from. Armies wear uniforms to know a foreign enemy from a comrade. Professionals like nurses, police, EMT, firefighters etc. all wear uniforms to let the people they are helping know who they are and that they can be trusted in a scary situation. What they wear matters. My dad was a firefighter, so I know that this is especially true for professions like firefighters. If they don't have the right protective gear, not only will they not be able to rescue someone, but they themselves will not make it out alive. They train with all that gear on because they must get used to all that extra weight. A literal burden has been put on them to rescue people and they need to carry it well in order to do their jobs.

While we are all unique, if we want to be a wonder woman who rescues others, we need to wear the right uniform and also recognize others who are wearing the same uniform. Unlike the Wonder Woman of the comics, you see, there are millions, if not billions of us. When you recognize other wonder women, you can acknowledge that you are on the same team and work together for a united goal.

Going back to the basketball analogy, a good team passes the ball to each other. Some members of the team may be great shooters, so perhaps you might pass the ball to them when they are free, but that doesn't mean each person on the team isn't valuable. Another person may have set a screen, which is a way of blocking the defense so that person with the ball can be free to shoot or go to the net.

Ephesians 6 says faith is our shield. Faith blocks the attacks of the enemy because it extinguishes those false claims that come our way. When we talk about faith, it is often on a personal level, but we can also have faith in one another. Like the screen in basketball, the person creating the screen has faith that their actions will cause the other person to score for their team.

As women, too often we do not root for other women because we do not recognize that we are on the same team. As women, we are notoriously catty, mean, and gossips to and about other women. When one woman rises in business in a man's world, there's even a term for how she often acts to other women trying to rise in the same field: the queen bee - she stings any other bee she sees trying to "invade" her territory.

Perhaps it's because traditionally men have been more likely to wear uniforms for war or sports, they recognize the value of the team. Many women are starting to embrace and spread the idea that we are #bettertogether, but historically it's been a long time coming. If we could recognize the power of coming together in unity, our force for good in this world would be unstoppable. Ecclesiastes 4:12 says, "Though one may be overpowered, two can defend themselves. A cord of three strands is not quickly broken." When we stand with one another, we create a much more powerful shield. From history, I recall that Roman soldiers would interlock their shields to create a huge barrier like a tortoise shell, which could then march together, protected from the arrows coming their way. In combat, their weakest point of protective armor was their back, so they would often fight back-to-back. As women, we need to join forces and "have each other's backs." We can be much more confident and go farther when we know we have a team. There is an African proverb that says, "If you want to go fast, go alone. If you want to go far, travel together."

The amazing thing about when you are on God's team is that even if you feel that you don't have a team of any people around you, you have an incredible shield around you. There's a worship song that says, "This is how I fight my battles. It may look like I'm surrounded, but I'm surrounded by You." That's an awesome image that we sometimes need to remind ourselves of.

If only we could see those angel armies, how great our understanding would be. 2 Kings 6:15 tells the story of the prophet Elisha being surrounded by an army. His servant was scared, but Elisha answered in verse 16, "Don't be afraid. Those who are with us are more than those who are with them." Verse 17 says, "And Elisha prayed, "open his eyes, Lord, so that he may see." Then the Lord opened the servant's eyes, and he looked and saw the hills full of horses and chariots of fire all around Elisha." Imagine if we were able to see the invisible! When you align yourself with the one who created the universe, we are in the majority. When you know and have that power, you can become a shield for others.

In the 2017 movie, Wonder Woman at one point becomes that shield so that the army can advance after being stuck in one place for a long time. She uses her arm bands to block the bullets coming her way. These arm bands that she wears have an interesting history. They were called bracelets of submission because, in Wonder Woman mythology, they were originally worn when Hercules had power over the Amazons. They are still worn today by the Amazonian women to remind them that if they forfeit their independence to men, their power will be drained.

Now I'll say for the record that I am a feminist in the sense that, as a woman, I care about women's issues. In writing this book though, I am not supporting any particular feminist agenda. The writers of the comic book hero do, however, have various agendas and some of the symbolism of who she is and the things she wears is not by any means what I am trying to get across in this book. I do think as women though, that we have, throughout history, forfeited our independence and it literally took away our power. It's incredible to think that just around 100 years ago, women couldn't even vote in a land where we value that "all men are created equal." We need to stop and thank the heroes that have gone before us that have given us and paved the way for the freedoms and opportunities we enjoy today. What role will we play in paving the way for future generations to come?

A hero should be humble, but a hero is never a slave. A hero keeps their ego in balance, however, through lovingly serving people. A true hero does something not for the glory, but for the good of the people they help. A Wonder Woman's power comes from remembering that although she is not a slave to anyone, she can lovingly submit and commit to rescuing others. Those with power who do not balance their egos with submission and humility often become the villains of the stories, only ever thinking of themselves and their needs. The bracelets show the power we have when we serve others in a mighty way and with a loving heart - and it warns us how our power is drained when that service turns into obligations, and we begin to feel enslaved by it.

Now that we've discussed your shield and jewelry, let's talk about shoes. I know there are a lot of ladies out there who like their shoes. People love their shoes so much, in fact, that the industry is valued at around 300 billion per year! Shoes are an interesting piece of clothing because, while they are necessary, they have evolved in a way that their shape and style reveal a lot about the wearer. If you are wearing flip flops, snow boots, stilettos, or sneakers, it tells a lot about your environment and what you are involved in. There was a movie in the '90s called *Sneakers*.[38] The movie actually had nothing to do with footwear and was really about computer hackers and codes, but there was a reference in the movie about how they could tell a lot about a person by the shoes that they were wearing. The main characters, played by Robert Redford and Ben Kingsley, would always ask about or notice the shoes someone was wearing. The shoes acted like a code that reveals your personality.

Now, I will tell you that I am not a shoe girl. I probably have about 10-15 pairs of shoes and most of them are sandals. I'm sure this tells a lot about me, but I found a pair of gold Reef flip flops in 2014, and I have been wearing them ever since... and it is now 2020 as I write this. I've bought multiple pairs and have worn out a few, but I keep wearing them. They are comfortable, simple, and go with a lot of outfits here in Florida.

Well, about six months ago, I made a last-minute stop into a shop for a quick pedicure while my son was at preschool. It wasn't a normal salon but a Chinese herbalist, but the sign on the window said "pedicures," so I went in. The woman not only gave me the best pedicure, but she told me a lot about my feet. She could tell that I wore the same shoes every day and that they weren't very supportive to my feet. I have since bought some new shoes with better support. I currently work from home and live a mostly casual lifestyle, but like that famous book about getting a job says, I needed to "Ditch the Flip Flops."

Ephesians 6 says, "to have your feet fitted with the readiness that comes from the gospel of peace." As Wonder women, although we physically may want to be barefoot and feel the wonder of the grass between our toes and the sand beneath our feet, metaphysically we need to be wearing shoes that "let us run with endurance the race that is set before us" (Hebrews 12:1). Let's just leave it to say that I don't necessarily think we should be wearing Wonder Woman high heels for this race, and it's obvious that the creator of the character of Wonder Woman was a man because no one who has ever worn heels would choose them for a race or a battle. So, in this analogy, the comic book character is not the best (although some of the original comics do show her wearing lace up sandals instead).

Our feet need to be metaphorically protected with shoes that don't just cushion ourselves, but ones that help us have the confidence that we can go farther to tell others about the good news of peace. Imagine for a moment that your country has been at war. Think back before cell phones. Picture in your mind ancient Greece, for example, being attacked by the Persians. Imagine you are in Athens and the battle is just outside your city in a battlefield near the town of Marathon. You are so worried - but suddenly, a soldier comes running up to you declaring Victory! You all rejoice knowing there will be peace for you. Then you realize this soldier has just run over 25 miles to give you this message of peace. And if you don't know the story or haven't figured it out by now, this is where we get the name and distance for the Marathon race.

We run and we train to spread the message that there has been victory. The good news is that Christ defeated death when He rose from the dead. That battle is over, and you can have peace. Many people don't believe this message though. They live their lives in fear and worry when peace is available to them. We can't force people to believe in this peace, but we can live in a way that shows them how WONDER-full it is to have true peace.

We all have our own unique personalities, and just like our shoes, our peace doesn't have to look the same. You don't have to be a barefoot hippie holding peace signs (although you can be). Your peace might be able to be shown off in the boardroom, the emergency room, the classroom, the kitchen, or wherever you may be found. When others are stressing and fearful, look at your feet and remember that while they may be invisible, you are a Wonder Woman and have super shoes of peace. Make it so others WONDER about that peace so that you can share it too.

Regarding the other items Wonder Woman wears, I can't say that they are exactly protective armor. On the contrary, as we can all picture in our minds, she is scantily clad. Her costumes have also changed through time depending on the illustrator and the decade she was in. While the Ephesians 6 analogies don't ring true, she does wear a few things of note as we wrap up this chapter. It may not be a helmet, but she always has her tiara, which signifies she is of royal descent. As a child of God and daughter of the King, we need to remind ourselves that we represent the kingdom wherever we go. As a princess we may wear a tiara, but there will also come a coronation day on which we will receive a larger crown as well if we are faithful. We wear the crown when we are mature enough to show that we represent the kingdom, just like a princess does not earn the right until she is old enough to understand her rights and responsibilities. It is something we also earn.

Likening our crowns to those from the Olympic games, Paul writes in 2 Timothy 2:5, "An athlete is not crowned until he competes according to the rules," and in 2 Timothy 4:7-8, he says, "I have fought the good fight, I have finished the race, I have kept the faith. Now there is in store for me the crown of righteousness, which the Lord, the righteous Judge, will award to me on that day—and not only to me, but also to all who have longed for his appearing."

Wonder Woman's tiara, like her belt and "breast plate," brand her to show who she is. She shows off her big WW that looks like an eagle flying and we know who she is. Whether she is wearing the American stars skirt or the Amazonian warrior look, we recognize who she is. While it may not be a perfect analogy, I have written these things to help us to recognize and bring out the warrior hero in ourselves and in one another. When we dress in different types of clothes, we often take on a particular persona. If I'm wearing a black power suit with heels vs. a Lilly Pulitzer dress in sandals, I'm going to feel and act in different ways. This is why people, especially children, love dressing up in different kinds of clothes. It lets us imagine and put ourselves into a particular role. We may not (and please don't) want to dress in a Wonder Woman costume, but each day when we get out of bed, we can imagine ourselves putting on our warrior gear. As we get ready to tackle the day, let's imagine our sword and shield and lasso of truth. Visualize the hero within you and she will emerge.

Reflection Questions for Journaling or Group Discussion

- Do you view other women as being on your team? Do you have a sisterhood of other women who all "have each other's backs?" If not, I encourage you to try to find your "tribe."

____

____

____

- How can there be power in submission? How can you commit to serving others in love without it becoming something that you feel enslaved to do?

____

____

____

- Are your feet fitted with the "gospel of peace?" In what ways in your daily life, can you show others that you have this peace?

____

____

____

CHAPTER Nineteen: A WONDER WOMAN HAS BALANCE

"Happiness is not a matter of intensity but of balance and order and rhythm and harmony." - *Thomas Merton*

Throughout this book, I have given some advice that sometimes seems somewhat contradictory. On the one hand, I have said it is important to be your true, authentic self and then in the next chapter I said to metaphorically wear your team uniform. So, which is it? Of course, it is both, which is why we need to learn the sacred art of balance.

The word balance comes from the root words *bi*, meaning two and *lanx*, which was a scale pan. The most obvious picture in our minds is a scale, where when the two sides have equal weight, it is balanced. Even though we don't use scales like this commonly anymore, we still refer to money being on a balance sheet, and we refer to it as a positive or negative balance.

Balance and harmony in nature is critical. The universe has a natural inclination toward equilibrium and there is even a law of equilibrium that states that when a system experiences a disturbance, it will respond to restore a new equilibrium state. I taught high school chemistry for a few years, so I apologize again if I'm taking you back to painful years when you had to endure this stuff. Unless you go into a science field, you probably never use it in real life - but I want to take this time to give you a real-life application so that it was hopefully all worth it. In case you can't remember, the whole reason you learned to balance equations was because there are these conservation laws in the universe that say matter and energy are neither created nor destroyed - they simply take different forms. When you balance the equations, you are trying to determine what the results will be when you combine two chemicals together. Depending on your goals, perhaps you want an explosion or perhaps you don't. The creators of fireworks want the chemicals to combine at just the right time and mix chemicals that will create beautiful colors and explosions. Otherwise, most of the time, we are trying to prevent things from blowing up. Certain chemicals, like ammonium nitrate, if they are not stored properly, can have devastating results, as seen in the huge explosion that occurred in Beirut, Lebanon in August of 2020.

We balance equations in chemistry so that we can perform experiments safely instead of blowing up the classroom. We want to try to predict the results of what will happen if we add a certain new compound to the mixture. So, the same is true in our lives. When we are debating about adding a new activity or thing to our lives, we need to weigh out the pros and cons because that new element will cause us to readjust our balance point.

As an example, my daughter recently has been wanting to ride horses. She doesn't do a lot of extracurricular things, so we decided to let her try it. The only problem is that the stables are about 40 minutes from my home - so by the time we get back, its nearing dinner time, which has caused us to stop for fast food drive-thru two weeks in a row. As one who values home-cooked, healthy food, this is not my ideal. But I also must realize that this may be the tradeoff for adding this element into our lives - either that or I need to prepare and pack a picnic dinner or put something in the Instant Pot at home.

So, you see - there is a tradeoff and a new balance point set. This is easy to understand when you are only adding one ingredient to the mix. But what if you are continually adding ingredients to the mix? What if you can't say "no" when someone asks you to do something. You're on the board of this thing and chair the committee on another thing and have this sales meeting. Whatever it may be, suddenly you have too much going on and you find you can't balance it all. My friend calls it "ramming," which means you're just going so fast - trying to push through it all and get it all done. But ultimately the term ramming means to crash violently into something, which is usually what ends up happening.

None of us wants an explosion to happen in our lives, but if we're not thinking about the "ingredients" we're throwing together in the pot, this could be the consequences. My daughter likes to bake without using a recipe. She likes to throw things together and see what happens. That's ok when you're a kid to some extent, and while they have occasionally been not horrible to eat (with a little advice from me), we've had to start telling her that her creations are just not that tasty. Following a recipe of someone who has done it before helps us to balance out the ingredients so that we don't have to learn by trial and error.

In music and in many other fields, when you speak about balance, we use the term harmony. When all the musicians are playing their parts at the right tempo, the piece sounds auditorily appealing. But what happens if just one of the musicians starts to do their own thing? Professional musicians fine tune their craft through continual practice and repeated habits. So too, we can find the balance and harmony we desire through practice. Each day you start to feel out of balance, take serious note of what it was that contributed to that imbalance and either eliminate that thing or find out what may be missing.

If an orchestra is not playing in harmony, it's highly unlikely that adding one more instrument will make it more harmonious. In contrast, the solution usually involves cutting out or narrowing things down until you discover the instrument that is out of tune or the player that is out of sync.

Those amazing people who can tightrope walk didn't start their journey far above the earth. Perhaps they started young on a wide balance beam and moved to a thinner and (finer) rope and then gradually moved higher and higher. There is a great documentary called, *Man on Wire*[39] that shows how Philippe Petit managed to string a wire between the twin towers in New York City and walked between them! Talk about faith!

I like to paddleboard, and the other morning it was so calm and clear that I went way out into the ocean - farther than I ever have. The water was crystal clear, and so I could see all the way to the bottom, which was awesome, but it also made me feel I was 50 feet off the ground. At one point my knees started to shake as a twinge of fear hit me. It made me think of the story when Jesus was walking on water and Peter got out of the boat and started walking on water too (Matthew 14:22-23). We can't even comprehend how he did this and the faith that he had to step out of the boat into these waters. When his eyes were on Christ, he was able to do it, but as soon as he started to be afraid, he began to sink, and Jesus told him that he had little faith. How much less is our faith when we won't even get out of the boat? We've all probably experienced times of fear at various points when we reach new heights. We're fine one moment and then a little voice in your head starts to shake your confidence that you are safe. Your body physically reacts with sweaty palms or a racing heart. The term "weak in the knees" is something that literally happens.

Just like in the physical world, fear can cause you to lose your balance in the metaphysical world as well. Although we can't see all the things that we are metaphorically and metaphysically juggling, fear can cause you to lose your balance, especially if you are walking a fine, high rope.

I took dance lessons when I was young and even did a little ballet and tap as an adult as well. When you learn to do turns like a pirouette, they teach you to have a focus point so that you don't get dizzy. You are supposed to pick a spot to focus your eyes on for as long as you can while the rest of your body is spinning. Your head remains facing that one direction for most of the time. I believe the current world record is two hundred *fouettés en tourne*, which is when you turn on one leg and the other leg kind of whips around to give you more momentum to keep spinning. Most professional dancers can do around 35-40, but a 7-year-old broke this record. A young girl also holds the record for the most turns in a single pirouette.

Children are often much more adaptable than us adults and their brains can adapt in order to not get dizzy when spinning. There are some adults, however, who have adapted their brains in order to spin as well. I had the privilege of seeing a whirling dervish performance while traveling in Turkey several years ago. These Semazens, as they are known there, perform a spinning ritual for a very long time. If you are not familiar with it, search online for a video to see what I am referring to. This spinning is done as an act of meditation, where you release the ego, focus on God, and symbolically imitate the planets around the sun (interestingly this was developed hundreds of years before Copernicus gave the western world the heliocentric model). Everything they do and wear is representative of their release of their lower self/ ego and their rebirth to truth. The word Semazen literally means "hearing and doing." Those who perform this practice aim to hear the subtle sounds of the cosmos.

It's interesting that balance in the body is controlled through the inner ear. I don't know if this was known in the 13th century, when the poet Rumi began this whirling tradition, but it's interesting how the ear and balance go together. We often get out of balance when we get distracted by the noises around us. We lose our train of thought and focus. (How many moms out there can attest to the fact that they can no longer keep one thought in their mind for very long. Even conversations get interrupted constantly and you find yourself saying, 'What was I saying again?') The Samazen are able to whirl because they have learned to take their focus off of anything in this world and they do not let their ears distract them or tell them that they should be a certain way. Their focus and alignment are with the Spirit.

I must admit that this is an area of my life as an adult that I need to work on. As a child, I could spin easily. Now, as an adult, I get dizzy when I spin my kids too long. I also get a little sea or air sick when my inner ear tells me that I'm not on solid ground. I've only been skydiving once, but my inner ear hurt so much during the free fall that I could barely hear for days after. Since then, it has hurt also when I have gone scuba diving, where you must equalize the pressure to maintain inner ear balance.

Maintaining balance under pressure is tricky. In scuba diving, you have to swallow and allow your ears to pop as you descend to deeper depths. Experienced divers tell you to go feet first, look up, stay ahead of the pain by equalizing often, and stop if it hurts. Spiritual analogies can be made here. When you are under pressure or know that you are going into a stressful situation, it's important to maintain your balance and equilibrium by looking up to the Source, jumping in feet first and swallowing often to handle whatever comes your way. If you go faster than you can handle, you will feel pain, but if you take it slowly and equalize often, you can explore the wonder of a new world.

If you want to go far, you must have balance. Have you ever experienced a time when your car got out of alignment? The steering wheel starts to shake and if you let go of the wheel even for a moment, the car will drift to one side. This recently happened to our car after we had a flat tire and had to replace one. The thing we failed to do was to get a tire balance. Because of this, the opposite tire got so worn down on one side that it also went flat. I learned my lesson in both cars and life: taking the time to balance will save you trouble down the road!

As a health coach, I use a tool called *the circle of life* to help clients visualize any specific areas of their life that may be out of balance. If, for example, you were to focus too much on your career but have no outlet for creativity, things might be ok for a while, but then after time, it may seem like your life is getting a little dull or "flat." – so you might turn to salty foods to give a little "spice" to that craving that you really have for more creativity. It's not that you need be perfect in every area of life, but in order to move forward, you need that circle to look somewhat symmetrical. In the next chapter, we'll look to see how we can practice this balance with consistency.

Reflection Questions for Journaling or Group Discussion

- Think about some ways that we as women can feel out of balance. Are you so focused on your children's needs that you are forgetting to form lasting friendships of your own? Have you been running on too little sleep or compensating with too much coffee? Have you been connecting with nature or spending too much time in front of a screen? Is your home a haven you enjoy being in or a constant source of struggle and anxiety?

  ____

  ____

  ____

- In what ways does fear make you "weak in the knees?"

  ____

  ____

  ____

- Look at the circle of life tool on my website www.wonderwomanhealthcoaching.com In what ways are you feeling a little "flat?"

  ____

  ____

  ____

CHAPTER Twenty: A WONDER WOMAN IS RELIABLE

"Accountability breeds response-ability" – *Stephen Covey*

Any sport that requires us to achieve a new balance point, like skiing or skating, requires practice for us to achieve a skill level where we don't fall when some hurdle comes along. With practice comes consistency and reliability. While we all like diversity and change from time to time, we wouldn't want to see a surgeon who has a 50% success rate. We don't want a superhero who *sometimes* shows up to fight the bad guy. No matter the field, we value experts who have a high rate of consistency and success.

Fortunately, surgeons or other skilled professionals have built-in systems of accountability. They must go through years and years of training, pass exams, and prove that they can do what they say they want to do. While this external accountability is great for professions like these, we don't always have this so formalized in our adult lives, and therefore, must strive to create it for ourselves. If you were to write down what you want to be successful at, you also need to check if your daily life and calendar is in harmony with those end goals. Your life now is the result of past actions. If you literally step on a scale, the number shown there reflects your actions of the past, going up or down depending on your self-indulgence or your self-discipline.

Psalm 26:2 says, "Test me, Lord, and try me, examine my heart and my mind." Proverbs 5:21 says, "For your ways are in full view of the Lord, and he examines all your paths" and Proverbs 16:2 says, "All a person's ways seem pure to them, but motives are weighed by the Lord." When you look at your bank account, you can see the results of your values - what you spent your money on, what you saved, or didn't save. At the end of each month, our accountant gives us a balance sheet to show what we have brought in and what we have spent. In our personal family budget, I can see what we truly value. Although we may *say* we value certain things, what we spend our money on may tell a different story.

Left to our own devices, most of us tend to eat too much, spend too much, do too much etc. - or maybe not enough, depending on our personalities. Setting up a system of accountability helps us to create habits that are in line with our goals so that we can have consistency in the progress toward what we want to accomplish.

As a child, we have built-in accountability in our parents and teachers, who instruct us when to go to bed, what to eat, and what to study. Our parents and teachers were there to guide us on a path in order to give us the best future possible. Those who have been trained to have self-discipline will fare better as adults because there is no one telling us now what time to go to bed, how much candy to eat, or to exercise. If you struggle with that motivation or lack of self-discipline, setting up accountability for yourself is one of the best ways to see consistent results. Whether it's using a pedometer to track your steps, using an app to enter your food intake, or having friends or a group to give you support and encouragement, measuring and accountability allows us the "ability to count" the progress toward our goals and the life of our dreams.

Groups such as Alcoholics Anonymous work so well because of their regular meetings and the people they choose to be accountable to. This helps to break the bonds from whatever addiction they may have been slaves to. I know that there is more to it, but how powerful is that? If there is something - an obstacle that seems unsurmountable or an addiction that has its grip on you, you must find accountability. Our willpower on our own is just not usually strong enough.

Accountability makes us look at each decision we make as having an impact on the scales. $5 may not seem like much money, but if I put $5 more on my credit card each day by buying a cup of coffee, at the end of the month, that's over $150. At the end of the year, it's over $1,800. Over the course of 5 years, that's over $9,000. If we began this analogy with, for example, a debt of $10,000 - in just 5 years, you could either have made that debt into $19,000 by buying that cup of coffee every day or you could have reduced your debt to $1,000 by taking that measly $5 and putting it towards reducing debt. I know this doesn't count interest and life is more complicated than this, but I'm trying to illustrate the power of our small steps over a length of time.

There are seasons (especially around the holidays) when you may give yourself permission to splurge. Life is meant to be enjoyed. Unless you have been called to be a celibate nun, you probably like to enjoy life. If we don't take time to celebrate and enjoy the harvest, then what is the point of all the work we do to create it? If, on the other hand, we splurge all the time, it creates imbalance and addiction.

We typically associate the autumn with harvest and abundance. For me, I have strong associations from my New England childhood with baking and anything pumpkin or apple. Anyone with me? Even though I now live in Florida, and we have to pretend its autumn when the weather gets to be a chilly 75 degrees, I recently got into a baking mood and made way too many ginger pumpkin cookies and pumpkin muffins. It was so much fun to bake them and smell those wonderful aromas throughout the house. The only problem was that they were just so good that I ate more than my share. That, along with the stress of doing virtual schooling with a pod of four children in my home during the Corona pandemic, had caused some pounds to creep back onto my body. I had created a group on Facebook called the "Daniel Fast Accountability" over the summer, where we had shared recipes and helped one another while doing the fast. I shared with the group that while I didn't really "feel" like doing another fast, I knew the scale needed to tip back in the other direction. A friend said she would do it with me, which helped me get the motivation I needed. We decided to do 40 days of the Daniel Plan, which is more moderate than the fast, but within that a 7-day detox, aptly named "Equilibrium" put out by Dr. Stephen Cabral. This detox uses the science of functional medicine and the wisdom of ancient ayurvedic principles to bring the body back into balance and harmony.

Detoxing isn't easy. This one involves two days of fasting and abstaining from anything processed even slightly and from complex carbohydrates, other than shakes that you drink that include all your essential vitamins and minerals. But just like anything difficult that is worth doing, the results are worth it. It's unfortunate, but our food and environment are filled with so many toxins. Our world and our lives have become so unbalanced.

You may or may not be familiar with the Hopi Indian word "Koyaanisqatsi." This word was used as the title for a film[40] made in the 1980s and can be translated as "chaotic life" or "life out of balance." The film also defines it as "crazy life, a life in turmoil, life disintegrating, or a state of life that calls for another way of living." Doesn't that define so much of our society? Most of us rush about - always "busy" - too busy to eat real, honest food that nourishes our bodies and supports our lives (and too busy to stop and WONDER what it is all for in the first place).

If we were to stop and take a moment to look around, we would be better able to take account of the life we lead. When it's all said and done and we leave this earth permanently, Romans 14:12 says, "Each one of us will give an account of him/herself to God." In Matthew 25:14-30, we read the parable of the talents that Christ told to his followers. If you are not familiar with it, I would stop and read it now. Depending on what version you read, it might substitute "bags of gold" for the original word "talent." A talent was equal to about 57 pounds and, in terms of money, it was equal to 6,000 drachmae (the money in Ancient Greece). While the parable doesn't specify if it was gold or silver, silver was just as rare as gold at that time, so either way to the hearers of this parable one talent basically meant like over one million dollars today. I've heard this story many times in church, but I don't know if anyone has ever really explained this value before. I often just pictured it as a coin, but in researching this, it has given me a whole new appreciation of this story. Imagine someone giving you 5 million dollars! What would you do with it?

In today's world we think of talent as some skill that you have… not a unit of measurement. If we look at the etymology, you will see an interesting progression: in the 11th century, it referred to a weight, but by the late 13th century it's meaning had shifted to: "inclination, disposition, will, desire."[41] When we think of our value today, so much of it is based on the talents that we have developed in our lives. Our income is equal in large part to the skills that we have and what we have done with what we have been given. Many people have a false idea that some people are just born with talent, but research has shown that this is simply not true. While a few rare geniuses are born, most talent must be cultivated through discipline and motivation or desire. We have all been given talents that are not to be hidden but are to be used and developed so that they grow. When we come to the end, do we want to be told by God that we were wicked and slothful? No! We all want to be told, "Well done, good and faithful servant."

While some people are truly busy developing their talents, I think so often many of us disguise our fear of letting our talents show with the "appearance" of being busy. We're "busy bodies," mindlessly stalking people on social media or alternatively doing activities merely for bragging rights on social media. Have you ever been talking with someone and found yourself saying that you are "so busy" and when asked specifically what you are doing you can't really answer? I must admit I have been guilty of this and known many people, especially moms, who respond similarly.

Before you go grocery shopping, don't you usually look in the refrigerator and cupboards to take "stock" of what you have and what you are running low on? We need to do the same in our lives. We need to take time to WONDER: What am I excelling in? What am I enjoying? What am I doing that needs to be eliminated? What do I need more of? Is what I'm doing nurturing the talents that I have? Does my calendar and my bank account reflect my priorities? What are my blessings? What are the areas that I need to focus on? Without stopping to take account of your resources periodically and measure your progress (or lack thereof), you may find at the end that you have not earned interest on what was given to you.

We think we are taking a journey in this life, but what if, at the end, we realize we accidentally got on a merry-go-round instead of a real horse? The Eastern religious concept of Samsara is the cycle of death and rebirth that exists in the universe. When you look at nature, you can see the cycles of life and death all around us. The seasons change and it repeats all over again. While a merry-go-round is fun, what if you were told, you could never get off it - ever. Suddenly, it would turn from something fun into a nightmare.

We all know various issues in our lives that seem like they keep coming back. Perhaps you thought you defeated some sin only to discover it had wormed its way back in again. Or perhaps you keep finding yourself having either the same issue with different people in your life or maybe it's just one person that you just can't seem to resolve something with. You're stuck, feeling like you're making no progress - just like wandering (which is the literal definition of Samsara).

If you look at the theme of the Bible and the history of the Israelites, it is a metaphor for us from being slaves to then being set free but still struggling and wandering - to then having the faith to enter the promised land. It really is all a cycle because the promised land is where they originally are said to have come from in the first place. The Eastern concept of Moksha that refers to emancipation/ freedom or enlightenment is like Moses leading the Jewish people out of enslavement and all the miracles that are performed along the way to bring them to their true home. I personally believe that Christ came to break this cycle for humanity if we choose to accept this. Just like a detox breaks the cycle of addiction from coffee or whatever else may be holding you in its grasp, Christ came to break the cycle of death. He showed us how to have true life now on this earth and everlasting life for eternity.

By taking an honest assessment of your life and finding ways to hold yourself accountable, you are following the way of Christ and putting to death the old sins, habits, and things that keep you stuck. You have been given talents -the potential that is inside of you, but you must be consistent in your actions in order to produce fruit from that tiny seed. In the next chapter, we will explore how to flourish and harvest not just fruit – but *good tasting* fruit that is the result of a WONDER-full life.

Reflection Questions for Journaling or Group Discussion

- Why is accountability so important? Do you have some people in your life that you can be accountable to for the goals that you set or the person that you want to become?

___

___

___

- What are your talents? How are you developing those talents?

___

___

___

- How does practice and accountability bring about reliability and consistency?

___

___

___

CHAPTER Twenty-One: A WONDER WOMAN HAS GOOD TASTE

Balance, peace, and joy are the fruit of a successful life. It starts with recognizing your talents and finding ways to serve others by using them.
-Thomas Kinkade

I recently learned the importance of the consistency of the size of grounds on the balance and taste of a cup of coffee when I accidentally bought whole bean coffee. Since we don't have a coffee grinder, I tried putting the beans in the food processor. While you would think fresh ground coffee would taste better than coffee that has been sitting in a bag, it turns out that to have a good tasting cup of coffee, it is important to have consistently sized grounds. My food processor, unfortunately, chopped some of the beans into larger pieces and some into a fine powder. I even tried to grind them in the blender, but my blender is also pretty old school - and while it makes a good smoothie, it was not able to grind it down evenly either.

Coffee, it turns out, is much more sensitive than I had realized. Those who take their coffee seriously, like my brother-in-law, make a science of creating the perfect cup. While I just pour pre-ground coffee into a percolator, he gets the water to the exact temperature it should be for the type of coffee he has purchased (depending on the location and altitude it was grown). I never thought I could drink a cup of coffee black until I tasted his creations. It's the main reason I try to avoid coffee, because I typically add way too much sugar and milk just to be able to swallow it.

Like that perfectly balanced cup of coffee my brother-in-law makes, we too can surprise people with our good taste. We don't need all the extra things that people usually use to mask bad taste. They will taste and see that our fruits are good. It's really hard to hide if you are out of balance. If you remember the old V8 commercials, they showed people walking tipped at an angle to show whether someone was balanced in all their fruits and veggies. It may not be that obvious, but ultimately what we have put into our lives shows out through the fruit that is produced. A wine connoisseur can tell if a particular year was too dry or too wet because of the sweetness of the wine. There are many passages in the Bible that talk about sowing and reaping because it is a universal principle and people in Biblical days were well familiar with the farming and the work involved in producing a harvest. Galatians 6: 8-9 says, "Whoever sows to please their flesh, from the flesh will reap destruction, whoever sows to please the Spirit, from the Spirit will reap eternal life. Let us not become weary in doing good, for at the proper time we will reap a harvest if we do not give up."

Today, the majority of us are less familiar with what it takes to produce good fruit, but when we taste something, we know if the soil was good or not. Have you ever had a tomato fresh from the garden or an heirloom tomato served at a nice restaurant? There's such a difference in taste compared to so many tomatoes that you find in the grocery stores. While farmers can control and produce many more tomatoes in greenhouses using hydroponic (ie. no soil) methods, there is the distinct soil flavor that is missing. Matthew 7 says that we will be known by our fruits. While some of us may be doing so much and producing a lot of fruit, we must step back and think about how that fruit tastes. What is the *quality* of what we are producing? Is our message too watered down?

When I was in college, I spent a semester at an organization called ECHO (Educational Concerns for Hunger Organization). They train individuals and groups for doing agricultural work in developing countries and help people learn about various and unusual farming techniques for differing environments. They often had speakers come in as well, and there was one speaker who showed us how we can measure the difference in nutrients between vegetables. They showed how the same plant that is grown in different environments and soils can range regarding their vitamin and mineral content.

While I titled this chapter, "A WONDER Woman has Good Taste," I fully acknowledge that taste in food, clothing, décor, etc. is a matter of preference. Beauty is in the eye of the beholder and what I may think is tasteful, you may not like at all and vice versa. While my daughter loves lobster, smoked salmon, and octopus, our young son would probably say that his favorite foods are still pizza and french fries, even though we try to feed him a healthy diet. Most of these preferences have to do with the seed that was planted at an early age. When our son was young, we were in a time of transition and probably ate out at restaurants too much and his palate became accustomed to having a choice of french fries far too often. As we get older however, we can choose different preferences if we train ourselves to step out and try new things. While I used to hate mushrooms, blue cheese, and spinach, I now enjoy all of them. Humans are unique on this planet in that we are the only species who gets to choose and adapt to our environment. We can learn to live almost anywhere, but the environment we choose to live in will determine the direction of our lives because *our roots soak up what is around us and create our taste.* You may have heard the quote by Jim Rohn before that "You're the average of the five people spend the most time with." There's also the saying, "show me your friends and I'll show you your future." While research has shown that your future is not necessarily shaped by just five people, all research does show that our networks influence us more than we know. While variety is the spice of life – and I love variety and spices, you also have to use the right spice at the right time. If I want to make a pumpkin pie and I use curry powder instead of pumpkin spice, it's going to turn out very different than my intention.

The fruit we bear or the harvest that is produced in our life will cause our life to carry on past our physical death. The fruit - and more importantly, the new seeds that are produced carry the genetic material for new life to carry on in this cycle. Jude 1:12 says to beware of people who are like "autumn trees without fruit and uprooted - twice dead." If we are uprooted, we die. No roots = no shoots = no fruits. Jeremiah 17:7-8 says, "Blessed is the one who trusts in the Lord, whose confidence is in him. They will be like a tree planted by the water that sends out its roots by the stream. It does not fear when heat comes; its leaves are always green. It has no worries in a year of drought and never fails to bear fruit." Jeremiah contrasts this to the man (or woman) who "trusts in man and draws strength from mere flesh and whole hearts turn away from the Lord. That person will be like a bush in the wastelands. They will not see prosperity when it comes (Jeremiah 17:6)."

While we may pause and think to ourselves - "well I know a lot of wicked people who prosper a whole lot more than me" - we have to look at what it means to be truly prosperous. It is referring to eternal prosperity. We all came into this world with nothing, and we will all leave with nothing - but some of us have a way of making the world a richer place to be while others take all the riches for themselves. The talents are not ours to keep. They are ours to invest and give back. Those who leave the world richer have taken the talents given to them and multiplied them out into the world, like a fruit scattering its seed.

Again, Psalm 1:1-4 says, "Blessed is the one who does not walk in step with the wicked or stand in the way that sinners take or sit in the company of mockers, but whose delight is in the law of the Lord, and who meditates on his law day and night. That person is like a tree planted by streams of water, which yields fruit in season and whose leaf does not wither - whatever they do prospers. Not so the wicked! They are like the chaff that the wind blows away."

We need to be *connected* in order to be *consistent*. If we are not planted with our roots in the right place, our leaves and fruit are likely to wither. While I like the look of potted plants and the fact that they can be moved if necessary, they are much more susceptible to withering if I forget to water them or if they somehow get too much rain. Their roots are all cramped up in a pot and have nowhere to go. They can't grow bigger than the pot they are given, even if they were meant to be a larger tree. About 6 months ago, I purchased some small citrus trees to go in pots in our backyard. They already had some fruit on them, so I thought they would be pretty and fun to harvest those fruits. Well, 6 months later and that fruit still never ripened. I'm not sure what happened. They got too much water in some heavy rains and then they split open before they had turned orange. Last week, a tropical storm came, and the wind was so intense for so long that it dried out the leaves and almost all of them fell off! I need to take them out of the pots - but I think I know that I will discover some root rot or perhaps I will find an insect colony attacking the roots. Because those roots are not connected and grounded, they are much more susceptible. A real citrus grower who needs to produce those fruits for a living would never leave their precious trees in pots.

2 Corinthians 9:6 says, "Whoever sows sparingly will also reap sparingly and whoever sows bountifully will also reap bountifully." While this is true, I want to take it a step further to say that we also need to be strategic and purposeful in our planting. If I throw my seeds onto the beach or in the middle of the road, I am wasting that seed because it will not grow. In Matthew 13 Christ told the parable of the sower. In verses 3-9 he says,

"A farmer went out to sow his seed. As he was scattering the seed, some fell along the path, and the birds came and ate it up. Some fell on rocky places, where it did not have much soil. It sprang up quickly, because the soil was shallow. But when the sun came up, the plants were scorched, and they withered because they had no root. Other seed fell among thorns, which grew up and choked the plants. Still other seed fell on good soil, where it produced a crop—a hundred, sixty or thirty times what was sown. Whoever has ears, let them hear."

A few verses later, he gives the meaning of the parable: *"Listen then to what the parable of the sower means: When anyone hears the message about the kingdom and does not understand it, the evil one comes and snatches away what was sown in their heart. This is the seed sown along the path. The seed falling on rocky ground refers to someone who hears the word and at once receives it with joy. But since they have no root, they last only a short time. When trouble or persecution comes because of the word, they quickly fall away. The seed falling among the thorns refers to someone who hears the word, but the worries of this life and the deceitfulness of wealth choke the word, making it unfruitful. But the seed falling on good soil refers to someone who hears the word and understands it. This is the one who produces a crop, yielding a hundred, sixty or thirty times what was sown."*

What this means is that each one of us has the capacity to choose what kind of soil we want in our lives. Are we going to cultivate our lives, and perhaps add some good organic material to create a place for that seed of faith to flourish - or are we going to let our hearts become hardened or let the weeds of the world kill the faith that we have?

Our hearts are the soil, and we can choose to cultivate seeds of gratitude, patience, joy, faith, or whatever we choose to plant. When those plants grow, not only do we reap the rewards of that mature plant, but those plants will produce seeds that can then be scattered into other people's "soil." If they are willing to receive it and tend to it, they too will grow seeds of faith and joy and love.

My parents have always been involved in supporting children in Haiti since I was a young child after the pastor of our church felt called to go and be a missionary there. They have seen children who had very little prospects go on to become leaders and teachers themselves, thanks to the education and support they received. They have also supported children in other countries as well, and somehow my mother became connected with a pastor in India who runs an orphanage for girls. The ministry is called "Fruits of Faith" and I personally know that this ministry and others like it, which I have the means to support, will ultimately produce the most abundant harvest for me. When I turned forty, I received photos of the girls in India holding up a big sign for me that said, "Happy Birthday Sis Adrienne." Although I've never met these girls and I live halfway around the world, I know that I am a hero and Wonder Woman for them.

I have had a heart for orphans and vulnerable children for a very long time. My master's thesis was even on the vulnerability of children whose mothers were infected with HIV/AIDS in South Africa. For a long time though, I had gotten distracted from my mission and the hero inside of me got stuffed into a little corner and forgotten. I got absorbed with my needs and the "good life" for myself instead of pursuing my purpose and passion.

I saw the photo of the girls, and it woke up that hero to remind me that this is to be the fruit of my faith and life. Maybe God doesn't have to be so blatantly obvious with you to show you a sign that literally says, "fruits of faith" (I guess He knew I needed a crystal clear indication to rouse me out of my selfishness) - but I'm sure there is something in you that you have been stuffing… some purpose that you have not been pursuing but that you know deep down is your true mission. Sometimes we need to work (or at least look) backwards in order to see forwards. As Stephen Covey says in his wonderful book, *7 Habits of Highly Effective People,*[42] habit #2 is to "begin with the end in mind." In other words, what is the harvest you ultimately want? Is it riches? Is it fame? Is it to make a difference in the lives of others? If you want to harvest a life that has influenced others, you need to first think about what and where you want to harvest and then start there. If you're living a self-indulgent life, you may be achieving success, but like Covey says, you don't want to spend all that time climbing the ladder, only to realize at the end that it was against the wrong wall.

The orphanage in India is currently only supported by a few individuals like my family and didn't have a website, so I have created one for them: fruitsoffaithministry.org. 100% of the profits from this book is going to support this ministry and other ministries that work with women and children, such as *Heart for Moms*, which is a local organization near me that assists single mothers.

If you would like to know more about supporting either of these ministries, please visit my website, youareawonder-woman.com for more information. Together, we can make an eternal impact and reap a harvest of good tasting fruit.

Reflection Questions for Journaling or Group Discussion

- How does your environment and those around you impact your life and your taste?

  ____

  ____

  ____

- Where are you planting your seeds? Is it where you want to see a harvest?

  ____

  ____

  ____

- Think of your life with the "end in mind." Where is it that you want to go?

  ____

  ____

  ____

CHAPTER Twenty-Two: A WONDER WOMAN IS GRACEFUL AND REFINED

Gracefulness has been defined to be the outward expression of the inward harmony of the soul. - William Hazlitt

As someone who has traveled a lot throughout the world, it still amazes me every time I see the balancing act that so many women perform every day. While we applaud the amazing feats of gymnasts on a balance beam or tight rope walkers (who certainly do deserve our applause), millions of women literally balance their daily burdens on their heads. I have seen women carrying tremendous loads of water - walking for miles just to bring it home to their families. They have such good balance and strength that they barely spill a drop of this precious liquid that we take for granted in the industrialized world. I once saw a woman carrying around fifty dozen eggs on her head in these large palettes. I swear that I'm not exaggerating and that it was the most incredible feat, worthy of being on a show like, "America's Got Talent." The roads are not nicely paved in these regions either, so one really needs to pay attention to where they are walking.

When you are trying to balance something, you have to stay focused and grounded. You also must have good posture. I don't know if I saw it in the movies as a child, but I would sometimes pretend to be a princess and walk around balancing a book on my head - because I guess that is what you do when you are training to become a princess. Royalty may not carry burdens on their heads, but they are expected to walk with incredibly good posture and grace.

As a child of the King, you too are expected to walk with posture and grace. We often think of grace as a pardon - as in we have been given amazing grace - or mercy and forgiveness. The term grace though literally means thankful and the Spanish word, "gracias" is usually translated literally as the English words "thank you." When you approach life in a posture or position of gratitude, your body is in alignment with the Spirit. You let go of the burdens and pain of unforgiveness and you walk lightly and elegantly through a room. Grace means that we have received favor and we extend that favor to others.

I want you to think of your posture right now. You may not have to carry a literal bucket of water on your head, but I'm sure you could write down a list of the burdens you are carrying. Although we previously talked about our baggage, I feel that there is a difference. Our baggage consists of things that we carry with us that keep coming back from time to time, while our burdens are things that we carry around constantly. Jesus says to us in Matthew 11: 28-30, "Come to me, all you who are weary and burdened, and I will give you rest. Take my yoke upon you and learn from me, for I am gentle and humble in heart, and you will find rest for your souls. For my yoke is easy and my burden is light."

It's interesting that even though we don't carry literal burdens anymore, we often feel pain and stress in our necks and back from these figurative loads. You may go to the chiropractor to help you temporarily align your body or masseuse to work out that tension, but unless you address the burdens you are carrying, those pains will keep coming back.

It's interesting to discover the ways the body can reveal to us hidden things that we try to ignore. Whenever I have some *dis-ease* or misalignment in my body, I try to discover the spiritual reason for that disease, and it usually reveals insights into specific thought patterns that I need to change or blocks that I have put up toward something.

Just like other things in nature, your body craves balance. The thoughts in your brain, our emotions, the foods we put into our bodies, and the environment or toxins we're exposed to all affect this balance. So many well-meaning physicians in today's world simply treat the body with prescription medications. While a medication may fix one area of concern, it often masks the underlying imbalance and is more of a "band-aid" approach. If you watch tv and have seen a commercial for any of these medications, you are very familiar with the long list of possible side effects that they are required to disclose. I'm not saying all prescription drugs are bad - some are very necessary if a disease has progressed too far - but we need to take a much more holistic approach to health care in the west. We need to filter or refine things down to their root causes.

To be refined means t*o reduce to a fine, unmixed, or pure state; separate from extraneous matter or cleanse from impurities*. Refining is not an easy process, but it is often essential in order to remove unwanted things from our lives. When we think of refining, we often think of something undergoing a process or being under pressure. Diamonds and precious metals have always been a symbol of refinement because they must emerge either out of pressure or undergo refinement in fire in order to be of pure quality. There are many Scriptures throughout the Bible that make this analogy. Isaiah 48:10 says, "Behold, I have refined you, but not as silver; I have tried you in the furnace of affliction." Malachi 3:3 says, "He will sit as a refiner and purifier of silver, and he will purify the sons of Levi and refine them like gold and silver, and they will bring offerings in righteousness to the Lord." The Spirit wants to refine us to remove the dross from our lives. The thing about gold though, is that after it has been purified and refined, it is extremely malleable and useful - but also soft and easily bent out of shape. To make jewelry, metalsmiths combine the pure gold with other elements like zinc, silver, nickel, etc. to make alloys. Although the Spirit refines us, I don't believe we are just meant to be pretty bullions with no purpose. Instead, He takes the gold and combines it with what we often think are the imperfections to make something strong and beautiful. We're not refined to just be like the famous "princess and the pea" story, who is just so genteel that even a pea bothers her under 100 mattresses.

The term, "refined" in today's world has sometimes taken on a negative meaning regarding foods because, in the food industries' desire to take out all the impurities, they have processed all the nutrients right out of them too. I personally try to avoid foods with the term "refined" on it. We all want our flours and sugars to be processed to some extent. It would be very time consuming to make a cake if I had to grind down my own sugar cane and grains - but why we still allow bleached flour in the U.S. is beyond my comprehension. It has been banned in Europe since the early 1990s.

So, there's even balance that needs to take place with our refinement and a refinement that takes place with our balance. The idea that we can somehow "have it all" is a myth. If we do, it's definitely not all at the same time. There is no way that we can balance everything and hold it all together. Researchers have discovered that the concept of multi-tasking is a myth as well. While you may be able to do a few mindless things at once, like knitting and watching tv (if you are an experienced knitter) - once you add in complex tasks, you simply end up doing both jobs poorly. It is much better to focus on one thing and do it well.

Even those ladies who carry things on their heads know that they can't carry more than one type of thing at a time. So often, we as women try to hold it all and do it all. We're multi-tasking all day, on our phones, checking emails while at our kid's sporting event. We're posting on social media, watching the stock market, the news, the weather and the other million things bombarding us with its "importance." The world wide web has connected us to everything everywhere, but like a web- we're spread too thin and fragile.

We need to refine it down. We need to take away the dross. We need to discover what is the important thing we need to focus on because, like I've mentioned previously, you can't focus on more than one thing at a time. There is a WONDER-full book called, *The One Thing*[43] by Gary W. Keller and Jay Papasan that basically helps you to refine down all your to-do's into one thing. They ask, *"What's the one thing you can do such that by doing it everything else will be easier or unnecessary?"*

When you identify your "one thing," your life may not seem in balance to others sometimes, but I would liken it again to a symphony or chorus. When someone sings the "harmony" part of a piece, by itself it doesn't sound like the tune we may be familiar with - but when you put it all together and you find people who can harmonize well with one another, you have a much more interesting piece of music. Instead of trying to do it all and be a "one man band," we need to learn to strip away the unnecessary and, instead, learn to play our unique part to the best of our ability.

It's interesting how the word "one" is a homophone with "won." When we focus on "one," we have "won." After reading *The One Thing*, I was at a charity event with raffles. For $20, you received about 20 tickets which you could put into different cups near the raffle item. There were several raffle items valued at around $100 - to $200, but there was one raffle item valued at $2,000. Obviously, there were more tickets in that one, so in the past, I would have spread my tickets out into the various jars for a "better chance" at winning something (which I usually never won). This time, however, I put all my tickets into that "grand prize" jar, and I also claimed it by telling someone that I always win. And I'm sure you guessed it by now, I won that prize!

I was interested to see if there were any books titled, *The Won Thing*,[44] so I did an online search and found a book by Peggy McColl, published in 2009. Because it had a sunflower on the cover, and sunflowers are my favorite flower, I felt like I should purchase and read the book. Because we are all unique, our "won thing" will be different for all of us - but winning the game of life isn't about stacking up accomplishments or accumulations. It's about appreciation of your life each and every day and living in the gift of the present. When we focus on one thing, it's much easier for us to find joy and pleasure in what we do because we have direction instead of being scattered in too many places.

McColl encourages her readers to come up with a unique formula or "recipe" for creating a fulfilling life, so I thought I would share here my "Recipe for a WONDER-full Life:"

Ingredient List:

- A cup of consistency
- A tablespoon of training
- A handful of harmony
- A pint of priorities
- A pinch of patience
- A spoonful of self-care
- A teaspoon of thoughtfulness
- A pound of presence
- A measure of mission
- A quart of quality time with loved ones
- A kilo of kindness
- A heaping of healthy habits
- A peck of peace
- An ounce of organization
- Gallons of God's grace
- A smidgen of success

- A cup of charity
- A bunch of balance
- A liter of leadership
- A dash of delight
- A spoonful of slow living
- A gill of gratitude
- A handful of humility
- A bushel of breathing room
- A cup of compassion
- A whole lotta love and laughter

Directions: Measure your words carefully. Fold together with focus and faith. Whisk together with praise and worship. Bake for 30 minutes of mindfulness at 365 days a year.

While this may seem like just a silly little activity, it shows us what we want and what we don't. I have nothing in there about being instafamous, making a lot of money, being the VIP at a party etc. If you want those things, I'm not saying they are bad; they are just not what I want to create in my own personal life.

By refining all the muchness down to one thing or "recipe," we can walk confidently in the direction of our dreams. We win when we are not waiting for some future success to be happy. We can be happy right now in this moment! So, ask yourself, what gives you the most joy? What is it that feels more like play that also gives you a sense of purpose? If you write down what you are grateful for in your life right now and take a posture of grace and praise to the "One," the "Won-ness" of your life will be revealed.

Reflection Questions for Journaling or Group Discussion

- What are the burdens that you are carrying? Either write them down as a list or draw a picture of yourself and write all the things that you are currently carrying. What could be eliminated or given over to God?

  ____

  ____

  ____

- What are some things you want in the "recipe" for your life? If there are ingredients that are missing, figure out a way to try to add these things into your calendar.

  ____

  ____

  ____

- What is one thing you can do this year "that by doing it everything else will be easier or unnecessary?"

  ____

  ____

  ____

CHAPTER Twenty-Three: A WONDER WOMAN IS LIGHT

"Darkness cannot drive out darkness: only light can do that. Hate cannot drive out hate: only love can do that." — Martin Luther King Jr.

As you learn to throw off the extra baggage and refine things down to only the important, don't you feel lighter? I love how in the English language light (meaning the opposite of heavy) and light (meaning the opposite of dark) are homophones as well. I have talked about being light and "being the light" throughout this book, so I'm sure you may be *wondering* how we are going to devote a whole chapter to it, but I obviously think it is that important.

When I first began journaling again a few years ago after a long hiatus, I had a journal that had the following words on the cover, "Travel Light, Live Light, Be the Light." Just like the light wakes you up in the morning, journaling awoke part of me that had been asleep for quite some time. If you currently are not journaling, I encourage you to pick this one habit up if it's one of the only things you get out of this book. Many successful people speak about how doing their "morning pages," helped them to get out of a funk, a writing block, or pushed them to a new level of understanding. Morning pages ideally are done first thing in the morning before you check any kind of technology. Writing long hand and in stream-of-consciousness style for at least three pages, allows you to realize and discover what is going on in the deeper recesses of your mind. You can also make it a prayer journal where you are writing down your thoughts to God or what you hear Him say to you in those early hours of stillness.

There is so much going on in your brain at any given moment. I think this is especially true for women, which is why I think journaling is often embraced more as a practice by women. When you do a "brain dump" you write down all the things that are "heavy" on your heart and mind. By taking out the mental and spiritual trash, it immediately makes the space in your temple feel light and clean. You can rest, knowing that whatever you need to do is now written down on paper. You don't have to be holding all this information in your brain. When you write things down in this way, it also sheds light on some things that may have gone missing or on something you didn't realize was even there. Just like when cleaning and organizing your home, you often find the thing you had been looking for forever the week before and gave up on finding. You need to *uncover* to *discover.*

In Luke 15, Jesus told the parables of the lost sheep, the lost coin, and the lost son. All tell a similar message of something being lost, the search for that missing object, and then rejoicing when it is found. In the coin parable, Jesus says, "Suppose a woman has ten silver coins and loses one. Doesn't she light a lamp, sweep the house, and search carefully until she finds it? And when she finds it, she calls her friends and neighbors together and says, 'Rejoice with me. I have found my lost coin.' In the same way, I tell you, there is rejoicing in the presence of the angels of God over one sinner who repents."

In John 8:12, Jesus says, "I am the light of the world. Whoever follows me will not walk in darkness but will have the light of life." Sometimes we like to keep our ugly flaws hidden. We don't want to expose our sins, but Jesus says that God sees us as valuable, like that silver coin. In any epic tale of hidden treasure, the hero needs to go on a search of discovery. It's not always easy, but it is worth it. Proverbs 2 says to "look for wisdom as if you were looking for silver and search for it as for hidden treasure and soon you will learn the importance of reverence for the Lord and the knowledge of God." It may not be obvious to all, but if you look at the cross in a different way, you'll see that "x" marks the spot.

When you find that treasure, you will soon discover that you too are a light. Although we may not have an actual source of light inside of us, it's like we've been covered in a reflective substance that shows God's light in the world, like glow-in-the-dark stickers. Jesus tells us in Matthew 5:14, "You are the light of the world. A town built on a hill cannot be hidden. Neither do people light a lamp and put it under a bowl. Instead, they put it on a stand, and it gives light to everyone in the house. In the same way, let your light shine before others, that they may see your good deeds and glorify your Father in Heaven."

One of my favorite things at Christmas is the traditional candle lighting service. If you have never taken part in one, I encourage you to do it someday. Everyone in the service is given a candle when they come through the door. Towards the end of the service, the minister will light his candle and then others will come and light their candle from that one. Then that fire gets passed on until the whole room is lit up. The thing about fire is that it doesn't lose energy when it spreads. It's not like one candle's fire is put out in order to light someone else's. It just keeps replicating. The same is true with the light of God. If we spread our light to others and they are willing to receive it, it only grows. The thing I've learned from many candle lighting ceremonies though is that the person who needs the light must come get that fire from the one that is lit. If you, as the lit candle, try to light someone else's candle by tipping it toward them, you'll just end up burning them with hot wax. Like the song, "This little light of mine," don't hide it or let anyone blow it out, you just need to "let it shine, let it shine, let it shine."

It's interesting how the Chanukah celebrations occur near the same time as the Christmas celebrations. Although I am not Jewish, we enjoy these celebrations, and we like to teach our children about different customs. The Chanukah story also revolves around light because they light one candle each night for eight days to tell the story of when there was only enough oil for one night for the temple lamps, but the eternal flame of the lamps miraculously stayed lit for 8 days. Chanukah literally means "Dedication" because it was a time when they were rededicating the temple after it had been desecrated and then won back. The Chanukah menorah has 9 candles - one for each night and a "helper" candle, the Shamash, that lights all the other candles.

We all appreciate the light even more when it's dark, which is why we all love the light of Chanukah and Christmas so much. Although most of us know in our minds that Jesus wasn't really born on December 25th, you may not know the history of why this date was chosen. Of course, as with all history, there are debates because we were not there to know the truth, there are many who believe it coincides with pagan holidays of the winter solstice, in particular the feast of Sol Invictus (the unconquered sun). Today, we are not an agrarian society and are not as familiar with the movement of the celestial bodies - but for people in ancient times, this was extremely important. Without electricity, winter was a cold and dark time of death and hunger. The "death" of the sun would occur at the solstice, the shortest day of the year. If you are paying attention though, the days don't really start getting longer again until December 25th. So, the sun (or son) "dies" on the cross (the horizon) and is in the "grave" for three days until it resurrects again (the days start getting longer once more). The sun is a representation of the son (again with the homophones). We celebrate the birth of the son of God on December 25th, not because that was the literal day of his birth, but because it is symbolic of what he came to do here on earth - be the light and the servant.

Most of us love the magic of Christmas because of the spirit of love that we feel. but of course, just like every religious holiday, the enemy has tried to distract us with commercialism. Instead of giving, some focus on what they can get. But Christ came to us to teach us the best way. If you are light, you can come even in the most unassuming package. You don't have to shout it from the rooftops. When you shine your light and do not hide it, everything will be drawn to it.

When you think about before the invention of electric light, or if you were out in the wilderness, the night was a scary time for people. A fire would give both warmth and security, as wild animals are usually afraid of fire. The other main source of light for people in the darkness is the light of the moon. When the moon is full and the sky is clear, you can walk even without a flashlight. The thing about the moon that we all know from elementary science classes is that it is just a big rock. It has no source of light in and of itself - but simply reflects the light of the sun. Just like the moon (although not as regularly), we can go through phases when we don't reflect the light as brightly or not at all. When the earth passes between the moon and the sun, this is when we see just a crescent or a new moon (where it is completely in shadow). This is a great analogy because, we too, do not reflect the Son as brightly when we let the world get in the way.

Romans 12:2 says, "Do not conform to the pattern of this world, but be transformed by the renewing of your mind. Then you will be able to test and approve what God's will is - His good, pleasing, and perfect will." We all want a life of purpose and probably have a desire to do God's will if you are reading a book like this one. This whole book is about transformation - and here is one of the keys in this verse: Do not conform to the pattern of this world. In other words, do not let the world get in the way of you and the Son.

Oftentimes, it only takes a slight shift for things to change. When we experience summer in the northern hemisphere, it is due to the way the earth is tipped on its axis. In July, we are actually farthest from the sun in our revolution. That axis shift, however, means more warmth, longer days, and the ability for more fruit to be produced. When we lean into the light, we feel its warmth. But the opposite is also true. When we lean away from the source of light and heat, we experience winter and more darkness. I never perceived this shift so much as when we moved to Florida from Vermont. You might be surprised by this, as the seasons are so extreme in the northern climates. Because we were surrounded by mountains and trees where we were in Vermont, however, you could never see the sunrise or sunset on the horizon. When we moved to Florida, however, we moved into a condo overlooking the ocean. It was so beautiful to see the sunrise and probably the thing that turned me from a night owl into an early bird. As the year went on, I was amazed at the difference of where I would perceive the sunrise in winter vs. summer. The change was much more extreme than what you imagine when you read about these things in a textbook. While we no longer live in that condo, I now have made it a ritual to go to the beach every morning for sunrise. There was a week that I missed recently due to constant rain every day (which is not common here). I was amazed even after a week, how it seemed like the location of the sunrise had shifted.

We may not notice shifts in our lives hour by hour or even day to day, but when we continue to shift and lean into the light, our days begin to lengthen, and we can accomplish so much more. In the book, *The Compound Effect*,[45] by Darren Hardy, he gives many examples of what happens when you simply and consistently shift your habits - either positively or negatively over time. One of the ways that he suggests bringing light to your habits is to write them down. By making a log of what you eat or what you spend or whatever habit you want to change, it brings awareness to it. It's like taking a flashlight and pointing it into a dark corner. Hidden things and patterns will be revealed. You need to "inspect what you expect" and *track* your habits to make sure you stay on *track* (again with the homophones).

If you have patterns in your life that you want to change, welcome to the club. This is not about achieving perfection. It's not meant to make you feel badly if you slip up. One of the songs that plays almost daily in our home and business is called, *Anthem*[46] by Leonard Cohen. The chorus of this song says, "Ring the bells that still can ring. Forget your perfect offering. There is a crack in everything. That's how the light gets in." I think if we recognize our cracks and our weaknesses, they can often become our greatest strengths. Perhaps there is one thing you have struggled with your entire life. You can't get past it because you haven't truly acknowledged this crack and allowed yourself to be exposed to the light of God's love. If you think about how a camera works, you open its lens to allow the light to come in and it takes in whatever image is in front of the camera to make an imprint. I would take a bet on saying that most people love their photos. If there were a fire or flood to your home, probably the one thing you would try to rescue, once your family was safe, would be your photo albums. In today's world, with things backed up digitally to the cloud, it's not as heartbreaking if you lost those albums - but there's still something we value so much in the way that a photograph captures a memory or an action that perhaps we can't even perceive with the human eye or remember.

There is much research to show that when a group of people sees something happen, like a crime for example, they all see and remember different details. They may even "remember" false information. But if the event was caught on camera, there is no disputing the facts. A photo can expose the truth the way a lighthouse exposes the rocks to a ship at sea or a headlight gives us the ability to drive at night.

Without light, we are blind, but if we see even the smallest amount of light, it can give us a direction to head in. Before the invention of the compass, on a cloudy night, sailors used to be lost at sea, but when the clouds parted, they could use the stars to guide their path. Light not only lets us see, but it literally gives us life here on earth. Without light, plants couldn't grow and produce energy through the process of photosynthesis. Without plants, we couldn't survive.

Ok. I think you get the point. We know the importance of light. So, this is the challenge to you: be light. Make it your goal. Do you have a goal to lose weight, make more money or achieve a certain level of success or fame? While those things are all fine, make them secondary to your goal to be light. Making this your number one goal will help you achieve your other goals as well because you will be going in the right direction. To be light, you need to reflect the light, which means you are leaning in the way you should go. We all know people who walk around with an aura of heaviness and others who walk with an aura of light. Some people claim to be able to see these auras. While I don't have personal experience with this, it's interesting that the saints in paintings were always drawn with a halo or an aura of light around them. It represents that there is something *wonder-full* about these people.

Ephesians 1:18 says, "I pray that your hearts will be flooded with light so that you can understand the confident hope that He has given to those He called - His holy people who are His rich and glorious inheritance (New Living Translation). Other versions say, "I pray that the eyes of your understanding may be enlightened." I love both translations. Don't you love the description of being flooded with light? Studies show that light deprivation leads to feelings of sadness and hopelessness. This verse says that light gives you hope. This was known long before the official studies.

Ephesians 5:8-15 says, "For you were once darkness, but now you are light in the Lord. Live as children of light (for the fruit of the light consists in all goodness, righteousness and truth) and find out what pleases the Lord. Have nothing to do with the fruitless deeds of darkness, but rather expose them. It is shameful even to mention what the disobedient do in secret. But everything exposed by the light becomes visible—and everything that is illuminated becomes a light. This is why it is said: "Wake up, sleeper, rise from the dead, and Christ will shine on you." Be very careful, then, how you live—not as unwise but as wise." In the next chapter, we will explore the wisdom that guides us.

Reflection Questions for Journaling or Group Discussion

- Do you journal? Have you every tried writing in stream-of-consciousness style?

___

___

___

- Are there things from your past that you have been trying to hide or bad habits you need to change? Take some time to let God shine a light on these things and wash away any shame or guilt. He sees you as valuable and wants you to live in the light and feel light.

___

___

___

- How can you reflect the light of God's love to others this week?

___

___

___

CHAPTER Twenty-Four: A WONDER WOMAN IS WISE

If any of you lacks wisdom, you should ask God, who gives generously to all without finding fault, and it will be given to you. James 1:5

That inner light that shines within the heart is the light of wisdom. The Bible tells us that the pursuit of wisdom is the highest goal that we can have. It is better than gold or gems. In Job 28, there is a wonder-full analogy about the pursuit for wisdom. You can read the entire chapter in your Bible or online, but here is a shortened summary.

There is a mine for silver and a place where gold is refined...But where can wisdom be found? Where does understanding dwell? No mortal comprehends its worth... It cannot be bought with the finest gold, nor can its price be weighed out in silver...the price of wisdom is beyond rubies.... Where then does wisdom come from? Where does understanding dwell?... God understands the way to it and he alone knows where it dwells...And he said to the human race,

"The fear of the Lord—that is wisdom, and to shun evil is understanding."

So, where and how do we acquire wisdom? As we look at this passage and other verses in the Bible such as Proverbs 1:7, they say this mysterious thing that the fear of the Lord is the beginning of wisdom. We spent a good amount of time previously looking at how to overcome fear and 1 John 4:18 even says "There is no fear in love, but perfect love drives out fear because fear involves punishment. The one who fears has not been perfected in love." So, what is this fear all about?

The fear of God is different from other false fears. It is a healthy fear, just like we have a healthy fear that keeps us from looking at the sun at mid-day or walking off a cliff. There is no "punishment" if we do those things - but there are natural harmful consequences. The fear of God helps us to live in a way that is wise because when we learn to follow the commands that God gave us, it helps all of us as humans to live a more *wonder-full* life. The commands are not here to keep us from having fun. They are here to protect us. When we tell a young child to look both ways when crossing the street and to hold our hands, it is not because we want to prevent them from enjoying life or punish them. It is because of our love for them that we want to protect their life.

Wisdom begins when we acknowledge that the One who created us knows us better than we even know ourselves. We see a tiny part, but God sees the big picture, the past and the future, and has all things under control. Therefore, when we let go of our control, our egos, and our small plans, we can better behold the greatness of God.

The ego, although it helps us to strive forward and better ourselves, tends to take things too far. All the "sin" in the world

- greed, lying, murder and the like are caused because of the false idea that "my" needs are somehow more important than "your" needs. It's the false idea of separateness. This is why all the "laws" for us to follow can be summed up in these two commands: love God and love one another. 1 John 4:20 takes it further and says, "Whoever claims to love God yet hates a brother or sister is a liar. For whoever does not love their brother and sister, whom they have seen, cannot love God, whom they have not seen."

In many ways, I like the concept of the Hindu word, "Namaste" because it acknowledges that we all have a divine spark. The word means "to bow" or "the divine in me bows to the divine in you." It's unfortunate that the Hindu caste system negates these words and places certain people as perhaps not as divine. The cows are treated better than some people. I never understood this. The work of Mother Theresa and other individuals have brought light to the plight of these people and the outcastes. The other problem with this word is that it might somehow make you feel like you *are* God. You may be a divine spark, but I'd like to see you try to make even the smallest thing out of nothing. The last time I checked, most of us can't walk on water, heal the blind with a touch, or raise the dead. The fear or awe or WONDER of God is the acknowledgement that there is One supreme being from which everything was made. When we worship idols or ancestors, we disrespect God - and He has made it clear how foolish this is. In Jeremiah 10, God says to the Israelites,

"Do not act like other nations, who try to read their future in the stars… their ways are futile and foolish. They cut down a tree and a craftsman carves an idol. They decorate it with gold and silver and then fasten it securely with hammer and nails so it won't fall over. Their gods

are like helpless scarecrows in a cucumber field! They can not speak and they need to be carried because they cannot walk. Do not be afraid of such gods, for they can neither harm you nor do you any good... idols are worthless. They are ridiculous lies!"

While it would seem like this would be something that "modern" sophisticated humans would not do, idol worship is still extremely prevalent, especially in the eastern cultures. I'm sure that most people believe their store-bought statue that was made in a factory is somehow just a representation of whatever god they worship, but then if that is the case why is the statue necessary? Will the god be forgotten about if the statue is removed?

Wisdom comes when we think about these things logically. As children, we believe in many things that aren't true. My goodness - all the lies we adults get roped into telling our children because of our culture! Last year, in a rather unwise moment, I found myself roped into buying an 'elf on the shelf' one day because my daughter came home from school asking why we didn't have an elf but all her friends did. She and her brother spun around saying, "I wish for an elf" because her friend told her to do that - and "magically" I found myself running out to the store spending $30 on a plush toy that should probably only cost $1. I know lots of people love this and the creators have certainly made a lot of money from it, but do I want to move it every night and then explain it away if I somehow forget? So many moms I know ask about if we do the "elf thing" and then groan. As if we don't have enough going on during the holidays!

This year I tried to do a little something intentional with it and I gave the kids "kindness" tasks like making bags up to give to the homeless from our car with some basic essentials and food. The only caveat with that is now, not only do I need to move the elf, but I also have to write little notes. Good thing I get up early! Anyway, my point after this little rant / tangent is that we often do things like this because of our cultural dictates. If no one else talked about the tooth fairy or the Easter bunny or Santa, I certainly wouldn't have done these things with my family. We are social beings however and want to "fit in" with what other people are doing. While believing in an elf or fairies may be something we do as a child, as we grow and mature, we need to step out beyond that. There are so many adults, however, that are still living with superstitious beliefs. They know deep down that a piece of jewelry made in China has no power to ward off the "evil eye," but still so many people purchase these and other "good luck" charms.

On the other extreme are the atheists who do not believe in a higher being at all. Psalm 14:1 says, "The fool says in his heart, 'There is no God.'" Also, Proverbs 3:7 says, "Do not be wise in your own eyes; fear the Lord and shun evil." Now, I don't claim to be the one person in the history of the world that has everything figured out. The universe is continually expanding (literally and figuratively) in our understanding of it. Although I'm clearly a Christian and believe the Bible is the inspired word of God, I'm not one who necessarily believes that every word is literal. I sure hope the book of Revelation doesn't happen literally, as it was written in symbolic and metaphoric language. Anyway, there are many different interpretations of the Scriptures and our understanding of the world, which is why there are so many religious groups and different cultures. I am thankful for the diversity of the human race, that we can all be different and colorful. How bland would it be if we were all the same?

I want to take a moment to share the ancient story of the blind men and the elephant. I like John Godfrey Saxe's version, who made it into a poem and popularized it in 1872:[47]

It was six men of Indostan
To learning much inclined,
Who went to see the Elephant
(Though all of them were blind),
That each by observation
Might satisfy his mind.

The First approached the Elephant,
And happening to fall
Against his broad and sturdy side,
At once began to bawl:
"God bless me!—but the Elephant
Is very like a wall!"

The Second, feeling of the tusk,
Cried: "Ho!—what have we here
So very round and smooth and sharp?
To me 't is mighty clear
This wonder of an Elephant
Is very like a spear!"

The Third approached the animal,
And happening to take
The squirming trunk within his hands,
Thus boldly up and spake:
"I see," quoth he, "the Elephant
Is very like a snake!"

The Fourth reached out his eager hand,
And felt about the knee.
"What most this wondrous beast is like
Is mighty plain," quoth he;
"T is clear enough the Elephant
Is very like a tree!"

The Fifth, who chanced to touch the ear,
Said: "E'en the blindest man
Can tell what this resembles most;
Deny the fact who can,
This marvel of an Elephant
Is very like a fan!"

The Sixth no sooner had begun
About the beast to grope,
Than, seizing on the swinging tail
That fell within his scope,
"I see," quoth he, "the Elephant
Is very like a rope!"

And so these men of Indostan
Disputed loud and long,
Each in his own opinion
Exceeding stiff and strong,
Though each was partly in the right,
And all were in the wrong!

MORAL.
So, oft in theologic wars
The disputants, I ween,
Rail on in utter ignorance

Of what each other mean,
And prate about an Elephant
Not one of them has seen!

While most people use this poem to say that we all have a little truth and not to be ignorant in claiming that they know best, my question to this poem is that if these were wise men of learning, why would they not have used their other senses? If they used their sense of smell, they would clearly know that it was not a rope or fan or a spear. If they listened to the sound it made, they would know that it was not a tree or a snake or a wall. If they chose to listen to one another instead of arguing, they would have been able to see the bigger picture. And lastly, if they had just been wise enough to ask someone who could see, they would have come to the correct conclusion. I came up with a little alternate ending to the story that I hope you enjoy:

And then a child walked by
These men who argued so adamant
"Since you are blind and I can see
I'll tell you, it's an elephant."

If you would use your other senses:
Your ears and olfactory
You can clearly understand it's neither
Snake, fan, wall, spear, or tree.

If you would simply listen
Instead of feuding in ignorance
You could understand the whole
Nature of these wonderful elephants

Then she went on her way
And they laughed, "This is all an accident!
What does a child know," they agreed.
"There's no such thing as an elephant!"

They walked away happy
Knowing there was no elephant for sure
Until each of them stepped into
A big pile of manure.

And so, the real moral here
Is to use your other senses
And listen to those who can see
Or there may be consequences.

Also, while the story of the elephant may be humorous and memorable, it is not a great analogy for God because the One wants to be known and communicates with us. In this story, the elephant seems to be silent and motionless as well, which is just not true of any elephant I've ever seen! God wants us to see the truth and not to be blind. Since the One is light and love, he wants us to be able to experience that. Psalm 146:8 says, "The Lord gives sight to the blind, the Lord lifts up those who are bowed down, the Lord loves the righteous." Isaiah 42: 67-71 says, "I the Lord have called you in righteousness; I will take hold of your hand. I will keep and make you to be a covenant for the people and a light for the Gentiles, to open eyes that are blind, to free captives from prison and to release from the dungeon those who sit in darkness."

A WONDER woman is wise - and that means using all your senses, learning and experiencing all that you can about the incredible universe, and being humble enough to know that you don't have all the answers. A wise woman thinks before she speaks. The book of Proverbs is full of wisdom, so if you are looking for it, I would start there. Proverbs 4:5-9 says, "Get wisdom! Get understanding! Do not forsake her, and she will guard you. Love her, and she will watch over you. Wisdom is supreme - acquire wisdom! With all your acquisitions, get understanding. Prize her, and she will exalt you. She will honor you when you embrace her. She will set a garland of grace on your head. She will give you a crown of glory." I love how in the Bible and in many other customs and cultures as well, wisdom is often referred to in the feminine. I like to picture wisdom as a wise old woman who comes alongside you and mentors you.

Since this is a book for women, I would be remiss if I did not mention Proverbs 31 - specifically verses 10-31. If you are not familiar with them, it is all about the wise woman, and I encourage you to stop and read it now. As you read it, be aware that there are some things that are not apparent when it is written in English. In Hebrew, it is written as a beautiful acrostic poem in a structure called chiasm, which is when a sequence of ideas is presented and then repeated in reverse order - resulting in a mirror effect. The one concept that is at the center and not mirrored is in verse 23, which is not about a woman but about her husband: All that she does brings respect to her husband.

While this may seem antiquated, I want you to understand as you read this that it was written as advice from a mother to "King Lemuel" on finding a good wife. While there is no historical King Lemuel, some have speculated that Lemuel can be translated as "belonging to God." If you are married, the number one thing husbands say they desire is respect. Whether you are married or not, I want you to read this chapter with the thought that your "husband" is God. In all that we do, do we bring respect to God? In various points throughout the Bible, we have been collectively referred to as God's "bride." I remember, before I got married, I prepared and worked on myself to create the qualities that would attract the kind of husband that I was looking for. We should be looking to do the same for God.

A.W. Tozer writes, "I believe that the reverential fear of God mixed with love and fascination and astonishment and admiration and devotion is the most enjoyable state and the most satisfying emotion the human soul can know. In fact, fearing the Lord means counting on our fellowship with God to make us happier in the future than anything else could."[48]

When the wise men came to visit the Christ child, they followed the light that guided them. Matthew 2: 10-11 says, "When they saw the star, they rejoiced exceedingly with great joy. And going into the house, they saw the child with Mary his mother, and they fell down and worshiped him. Then, opening their treasures, they offered him gifts, gold and frankincense and myrrh." If we are to be wise like these men, we too must bring our gifts and worship Him.

Reflection Questions for Journaling or Group Discussion

- Why is the fear of God the beginning of wisdom? How is this different from other types of fear?

____

____

____

- Think of all the unwise things you do because of social norms or cultural dictates that don't really make sense. What could you eliminate?

____

____

____

- Read Proverbs 31. In what ways could you apply this to the modern woman? How can we live a life of wisdom?

____

____

____

CHAPTER Twenty-Five: A WONDER WOMAN IS A WORSHIPER

"When the music fades and all is stripped away, and I simply come. Longing just to bring something that's of worth that will bless your heart. I'll bring you more than a song, for a song in itself is not what you desire. You look much deeper within - to the way things appear - you're looking into my heart. I'm coming back to the heart of worship. It's all about you. It's all about you, Jesus." – Matt Redman

The above lyrics were written by Matt Redman after his pastor did a somewhat radical thing and took the sound system and "worship" band away for a period of time. You see, he realized that the focus had turned too much to the wrong thing. It had become about the music and not about the Creator of that music.

So often in churches, worship is defined by a particular music style - some churches prefer more "traditional" hymns while others appeal to those people who like to rock out with drums and guitars. In some houses of worship, there is no music at all and in others, people do not even speak but their worship is in complete silence. Although music can be a tool for worship, so can art, dance, studying, walking on the beach, looking at the stars, serving others and much more. Our worship is any act where we stand (or bow or whatever position we choose) in wonder for the Creator of this amazing universe.

The word worship comes from "worth ship," the root "ship" meaning quality or condition - and if you look back further, it is also related to the word "shape." So, worship is the state or condition of being worth value, and the figurative shape of our hearts determines what we value. Here in Palm Beach where I live, we have a famous street called Worth Avenue, where everyone comes to shop the best and most expensive brands like Chanel and Tiffany's, along with high end art galleries, jewelry stores, and even the rare bookstore that my husband and I own. At the end of Worth Avenue is a clock tower, which overlooks the ocean. I often like to photograph the tower at sunrise because it stands in stark contrast to the light around it. For me, it stands as a symbol of the time we have here on this earth and a question to us of what we really value or what we deem "Worthy." As we talked about in the chapter on time, whatever we truly hold to be worthy or whatever our priorities are, we will spend time and energy toward.

We all worship something. We all deem something worthy of our time and energy - even if it's tv or social media. And whatever we worship is our god. David Foster Wallace once said the following during a commencement speech:[49]

"Here's something else that's weird but true: in the day-to-day trenches of adult life, there is actually no such thing as atheism. There is no such thing as not worshipping. Everybody worships. The only choice is what we

get to worship. And the compelling reason for maybe choosing some sort of God… is that pretty much anything else you worship will eat you alive. If you worship money and things, if they are where you tap real meaning in life, then you will never have enough, never feel you have enough. It's the truth. Worship your body and beauty and sexual allure and you will always feel ugly. And when time and age start showing, you will die a million deaths before they finally grieve you…. Worship power, you will end up feeling weak and afraid, and you will need ever more power over others to numb you to your own fear. Worship your intellect, being seen as smart, you will end up feeling stupid, a fraud, always on the verge of being found out."

While I don't know what Wallace believed or what you may believe about God, I know that I would personally like to focus my life/ value/ worship on the One who created me instead of another created thing. In *The Purpose Driven Life* by Rick Warren, he makes the analogy that "if you were given an invention you hadn't seen before, you wouldn't know its purpose. Only the creator or the owner's manual could reveal its purpose…. It is only in God that we discover our origin, our identity, our meaning, our purpose, our significance, and our destiny. Every other path leads to a dead end![50]"

Like Wonder Woman's Diana who was sculpted from clay, we too have a sculptor. You may view your life like clay - with layers continually being added until the masterpiece is revealed. Or perhaps you see yourself more like a marble statue - with pieces being chipped away until the true identity is exposed. Either way, we have to let the Creator do this work. We cannot do it ourselves.

Whatever we value, we sacrifice for. We are willing to pay the price because we deem it worthy. If we think a handbag is worth it, we literally will trade in thousands of dollars (which represents time that we or someone else spent working) for that item. If we value our family, we sacrifice not having other things, like perhaps that handbag, to spend that time with them instead.

Sacrifice and worship go hand in hand because when we sacrifice, we give of something to receive something better. While, fortunately, we don't offer animal sacrifices in our worship, I think that God wanted to teach the ancient peoples this important concept. We all sacrifice things - but sometimes our sacrifices aren't worth anything if they are done for the wrong reason. You see, the action of our sacrifice shows what we truly value. We may say we value something, but unless we show it in our actions through sacrifice, those words are meaningless.

We often worship what or who we admire or marvel at. We look at that person or thing as miraculous. Perhaps it's a sports player who can dunk the ball or the actress who can play a part so well that you think they really are their character. The old English "Wundrian," which the word wonder comes from, means *to be astonished, admire, or magnify*. When we wonder and are amazed by something, we magnify that thing in our lives. Like a magnifying glass makes something look bigger when we focus on it, so our wonder and worship makes whatever that thing is big in our lives.

The thing is that if you fill your life with anything other than the infinite then that finite thing will take up space in your life and consume you. But if you begin to shift your focus to the infinite, you begin to expand and grow because you are drinking from the well of life that will never end. We have a choice of where we focus our wonder and worship. My question to you is do you want to stay the same or do you want to expand and transform into the true WONDER woman you were born to be? If you fill your life with small things and small pleasures and the same old same old, you're missing out on the incredible journey of life that has already been given to you.

In John 4, the story is told about a Samaritan woman who Jesus met at the well of Jacob. Samaritans were people who were not liked by the Jews, but Jesus went there and spoke to her in a time when men didn't speak to women - especially those like her. To many, she was looked at as a sinner - someone who had been married five times and currently living with another man. Jesus spoke to her even though he knew her past and said, "Everyone who drinks this water will be thirsty again. The water that I will give him will become in him a spiring of water welling up to eternal life." If we fill ourselves with anything other than the eternal, we will always feel lacking - always wanting more. But if we drink from the well of life, we will be whole. We will be WELL. We will have true "well-th".

There's a lot of talk in today's culture about wellness, which is a great shift from simply looking at fixing disease. Putting good foods in our bodies and exercising certainly helps us to be well, but I believe if we want true wellness, we need to drink from the well of life and eat the bread of life. In John 6:35, Jesus again says, "I am the bread of life; whoever comes to me shall not hunger and whoever believes in me shall never thirst. When we fill our lives with the WONDER of the ONE we have WON. We are filled with love and light that makes us expand and ascend to places we never dreamed of.

When you look across cultures, when people win a game or are victorious, they naturally put their hands up outstretched and look up. Some people have speculated that if you simply make this motion even when you have not won something, it will make you feel like a winner and more powerful. While some people make a fist when winning, notice the difference when you open your palms up wide, look up, and smile. Try it now if you are able. What I realized when I was trying this one day, is that this looks a lot like the position many people make in some churches when they worship.

This is how they worshipped in the church that I grew up going to. I never wanted to raise my hands though when I was a child because in my young mind it somehow also looked like Christ's hands outstretched on the cross, and I was too young to die. I remember the moment I believe I gave my life to the Lord though. It wasn't in a repeated prayer said out loud. It was in a moment that I decided to lift my hands in worship. I spoke to God and said, "I don't want to die, but I know that you died so that I could live, and I want to live for you."

Christ's outstretched arms on the cross was the biggest power pose in HIS-story. When we realize the sacrifice that was made so that we can have life, we realize the worth of our lives and we live in such a way in which every moment is miraculous.

Reflection Questions for Journaling or Group Discussion

- What are you worshipping or sacrificing for? Is it really worth it?

  ____

  ____

  ____

- How can pausing to wonder help you magnify the things that are truly worth our worship?

  ____

  ____

  ____

- How does the living water that Christ gave us truly give us wellness?

  ____

  ____

  ____

CHAPTER Twenty-Six: A WONDER WOMAN PAYS ATTENTION

"The beauty and mystery of this world only emerges through affection, attention, interest and compassion . . . open your eyes wide and actually see this world by attending to its colors, details and irony."
— Orhan Pamuk

Throughout this book, we have talked about paying attention, but I want to unpack this one final time to leave you with some closing thoughts for going forward from here. The word attention means to "give heed to" or literally "to stretch toward," from *ad* "to, toward" + *tendere* "stretch." We use the word "pay" with the word attention most of the time. Going back to the last chapter on worth and worship, I want you to understand that your attention = your values = your worship = your future. Wherever and whatever you focus on and pay attention to is the direction that your life will go. Or as the saying says, "Energy flows where attention goes."

The problem is that we live in a world where attention deficit disorder is on the rise. We're bombarded by media, distractions, junk food, amusements, toxic chemicals and more - and it's leading us to live lives where we're spinning in circles with no direction. We need to slow down and pay attention to the ordinary miracles all around us. There's a song sung by Sarah McLachlan called *Ordinary Miracle*[51] that reminds us that everything around us is a miracle if we just stop and take a look at the seed growing, the rain falling, and the fact that we just wake up every morning. I have this song set as my ring tone on my phone to constantly remind me of the gift that we have been given.

When you look up the word *wonder* in the Bible, it is often used to mean miraculous. The Hebrew word מוֹפֵת (mopheth) can be translated to mean wonder, marvel, sign, miracle, symbol or really anything uncomprensible. This word is pronounced "mo-faith," which reminds me that when I come across something I don't understand, I just need to have "more faith" to see the miracle that will come out of the situation. When Mary and Joseph had to travel to Bethlehem when she was 9 months pregnant in order to follow a crazy *census* ruling, it didn't make *sense* in the physical realm. For all us moms out there, we know how uncomfortable those last few days are. Imagine riding a donkey over about 90 miles of hills through deserts and forests of wild animals and bandits. This trip would normally take around 5 days, but probably took longer since Mary was pregnant. Then they finally reach a destination only to find that all the hotels were fully booked. It didn't make sense, and yet all this fulfilled a prophecy in Micah 5:2 that the Messiah would be born in Bethlehem.

Another Hebrew word for wonder is אֶלֶפ, which is pronounced peh'-leh, and is the word used in Isaiah 9:6: "For to us a child is born, to us a son is given, and the government will be on his shoulders, And he will be called, *Wonderful* Counselor, Mighty God, Everlasting Father, Prince of Peace." This word is also used in Psalm 77:11-14 when it says, "I shall remember the deeds of the Lord; I will certainly remember Your WONDERS of old. I will meditate on all Your work, And on Your deeds with thanksgiving. Your way, God, is holy; What god is great like our God? You are the God who works WONDERS; You have made known Your strength among the peoples."

When you live a life practicing being in the present, meditating on the wonderful works of God, each moment of the future will become better and better. When you pay attention, when you breathe deeply, and when you act in love, gratitude, non-judgement, and forgiveness, life becomes this incredible, WONDERous journey.

We all know that old Chinese proverb, "a journey of 1,000 miles begins with a single step." When we start paying attention to the step we're on, it starts us moving in the direction of our dreams instead of spinning in circles. When we pay attention to the amazing gift of the natural world that God has given to us, it opens our eyes to the infinite power that we have access to daily. When we pay attention to our bodies and listen to the signs that it is trying to tell us, we can become healthy, vibrant, and ready to serve the world.

Psalm 139:13-14 says, "For you created my inmost being; you knit me together in my mother's womb. I praise you because I am fearfully and WONDERFULLY made; your works are WONDERFUL, I know that full well." God knows and created every single one of your over 30 trillion cells. Your heart began beating just 3 weeks after you were conceived, and it has beat to its own rhythm ever since that time. God designed you so that you never have to think about that heartbeat – and yet I want us to pay attention to that heartbeat. What are the things that excite you and make you feel truly alive and WONDERFUL?

In the original Hebrew the word "wonderfully" in this verse means unique and set apart. You were made for a purpose to leave your unique fingerprint on the world. As we travel on this journey, however, our fingerprints can be lost in the sands of time if we do not pay attention to *where* we put our attention. We can work building our castles, but if they are made of sand, they will fall.

In Matthew 7: 24-27 Jesus says, "Everyone then who hears these words of mine and does them will be like a wise man who built his house on the rock. And the rain fell, and the floods came, and the winds blew and beat on that house, but it did not fall, because it had been founded on the rock. And everyone who hears these words of mine and does not do them will be like a foolish man who built his house on the sand. And the rain fell, and the floods came, and the winds blew and beat against that house, and it fell, and great was the fall of it."

If we are not grounded on the rock of God, all our strivings will wash away. This lesson was vividly given to me by God one day when I was walking on the beach. Like the old poem, "Footprints on the Sand," I call "Footprints in the Sand for a New Millenium."

One day a girl had a vision. As she was walking along the beach, across the sand flashed words from our generation. Words like striving, money, pride, busyness, clothes, and followers. As she looked back on her footprints, they had disappeared… washed away by the waves on the sand.

All those words - the things that we spend time on - were washed away. They were written on sand and never made a lasting impact. It was like we were never here.

This really troubled the girl, so she asked the Lord about it. "Is there anything to do about this? Are we a lost generation? He whispered back, "My precious child, I love you and came to cleanse the world of the things that don't matter and to make all things new and fresh."

Then she saw a new set of words before her. Words like fear, comparison, anger, limitation, and pain. He said, "If only you will give these to me, I will wash them away forever."

Then he told her to climb up to the rock. It took her awhile to get there, but when she reached the top she found words like faith, joy, love, freedom, and purpose. And then it began to rain. When the storm had passed, a rainbow appeared and the light from the sun showed the words even larger than they were before. "My child" He said, "If you focus on the things that matter and write them on the solid rock of my being, I will expand them and make them last forever. Then she looked back and saw her footprints in the rock.

Psalm 40: 1-5 says, *"I waited patiently for the Lord; he turned to me and heard my cry. He lifted me out of the slimy pit; out of the mud and mire; he set my feet on a rock and gave me a firm place to stand. He put a new song in my mouth, a hymn of praise to our God. Many will see and fear the Lord and put their trust in him. Blessed is the one who trusts in the Lord, who does not look to the proud, to those who turn aside to false gods. Many, Lord my God, are the WONDERS you have done, the things you planned for us. None can compare with you; were I to speak and tell of your deeds, they would be too many to declare."*

The word attention is related to the word attend, which means *to be present, to listen, give care, or serve.* The day I turned 16, I got my first job serving or "waiting" on tables at a restaurant and did this throughout high school and catered during college, so I know a decent amount about the service industry. When you wait on a table, you need to pay attention to them, get their order correct, and make sure that their meal comes out in a timely fashion. We've probably all experienced a time when a waiter or waitress was clearly distracted and didn't get the order right. In our world of distraction, are we missing our orders for our mission because we are not in a position of waiting on Him?

Like the verse says, if we want to be pulled up with our feet on the rock, it starts with waiting *patiently* on the Lord. This is my verse for the upcoming year. Each year, the ladies in my Bible study each choose a word and a verse and share them with one another. Whatever verse the Lord guides us to grounds and guides us when we don't know which direction to head in. Each day going forward I want to ask myself the question: Am I paying attention to the WONDER all around me and sharing that WONDER so that God may be glorified? These are the footprints I want to leave in this life. What are yours?

One of my favorite poets is Mary Oliver, who spent her life writing about the miraculous natural world. In one of her most famous poems, called *The Summer Day*,[52] she writes:

> *Tell me, what is it you plan to do*
> *with your one wild and precious life?*

And so too, we must ask ourselves this question. I don't know what your story has been. Perhaps it has been tragic. Perhaps it has been messy. The great thing is that all those things that have happened in your past have given you strength for the future if you are able to learn from mistakes or forgive those who have hurt you. Your *mess* can become your *message* to help others. You can use whatever pain you have had to help others recover from that pain as well. There is a hero inside you that is just waiting to emerge if you have the courage and confidence to let her out because YOU ARE A WONDER WOMAN.

Reflection Questions for Journaling or Group Discussion

- What are you paying attention to? What is your dominant thought most of the time?

  ____

  ____

  ____

- What does it mean to wait on the Lord?

  ____

  ____

  ____

- How can the messy things in your life that you have overcome turn into your message to help others and be a hero for them?

  ____

  ____

  ____

Author's Note

I sincerely hope you have enjoyed *You are a Wonder Woman.* If you did, please share it with those you know and consider leaving me a 5 star review on Amazon.com. It is my first published book, so if you have any other feedback or questions, I would request that you contact me first directly at mail@wonderwomanhealthcoaching.com.

You can also visit wonderwomanhealthcoaching.com and youareawonderwoman.com for free resources that accompany this book. My hope is that you would connect with a tribe of women and use these as a launching pad to foster discussion and accountability. Each one of us is both a masterpiece and a work in progress at the same time. We need one another to help each other grow and thrive.

100% of the profits from this book are going to fund ministries that assist women and children, such as the orphanage in India that I support, www.fruitsoffaithministry.org. By purchasing this book, you have been a part of bringing the good news of God's love to those who need it in a tangible way. Thank you to all you amazing Wonder Women!

Connect with Me

https://www.instagram.com/wonderwomanhealthcoaching/

https://www.facebook.com/wonderwomanhealthcoaching

ENDNOTES

1 Armstrong, Louis. What a Wonderful World. https://www.azlyrics.com/lyrics/louisarmstrong/whatawonderfulworld.html. Accessed May 17, 2020.

2 Carey, Mariah. Hero. https://www.youtube.com/watch?v=q9BN0zyXAVQ Accessed December 19, 2020

3 The Incredibles. Directed by Brad Bird. Buena Vista Pictures, 2004.

4 Up. Directed by Pete Doctor, Walt Disney Pictures, 2009.

5 Sebastian Cabot, Phil Harris. The Bare Necessities. https://www.lyricfind.com/ Accessed May 19, 2020.

6 Warren, Rick, et al. The Daniel Plan: 40 Days to a Healthier Life Zondervan, 2013.

7 Hyman, M. (2010). The Ultramind solution: Fix your broken brain by Healing your body first; the simple way to Defeat Depression, overcome anxiety, and sharpen your mind. Scribner.

8 Amen, Daniel G. Change Your Brain, Change Your Life: The Breakthrough Program for Conquering Anxiety, Depression, Obsessiveness, Anger, and Impulsiveness. New York: Three Rivers Press, 2000. Print.

9 Wojcicki, E. (2019). How to raise successful people: Simple lessons for radical results. Houghton Mifflin Harcourt.

10 Lythcott-Haims, Julie. How to Raise an Adult: Break Free of the Overparenting Trap and Prepare Your Kid for Success First edition., Henry Holt and Company, 2015.

11 Billington, Ian. "The Physics of the Acoustic Guitar." (http://ffden-2.phys.uaf.edu/211.web.stuff/billington/main.htm), 1999, (http://ffden-2.phys.uaf.edu/211.web.stuff/billington/main.htm). Accessed 12 July 2020.

12 Seasons of Love. Songwriters: Larson Jonathan D, lyrics © Universal Music Corp., Finster & Lucy Music Ltd. Co.

13 Chapman, G. D., &; Green, J. (2017). The 5 love languages: The secret to love that lasts. Northfield Publishing.

14 Attr. Dallan Forgaill, 8th Century. Translated by Mary Byrne, 1905 and Eleanor Hull, 1912. http://openhymnal.org/Lyrics/Be_Thou_My_Vision-Slane.html Accessed October 17, 2020.

15 A magic paint brush - the story of Ma Liang. http://usa.chinadaily.com.cn/culture/2011-03/17/content_12187878.htm. Accessed July 24, 2020.

16 Bunyan, John, 1628-1688. The Pilgrim's Progress: from This World to That Which Is to Come. Philadelphia; Chicago :S.I. Bell, 1891.

17 The Gods Must Be Crazy. Directed by Jamie Uys. C.A.T. Films, 1980.

18 Hollis, Rachel. *Girl, Wash Your Face*. Thomas Nelson, 2018.

19 https://www.allmusicals.com/lyrics/chittychittybangbang/therosesofsuccess.htm

20 Kondō, Marie. The Life-changing Magic of Tidying Up: The Japanese Art of Decluttering and Organizing. Berkeley: Ten Speed Press, 2014.

21 Duhigg, Charles. The Power of Habit. Random House Books, 2013.

22 I Feel Pretty. Directed by Marc Silverstein and Abby Kohn. STX Films, 2018.

23 Leaf, Caroline. Switch On Your Brain: The Key to Peak Happiness, Thinking, and Health [Paperback]. Baker Books, 2015.

24 Leaf, Caroline. Think and Eat Yourself Smart: A Neuroscientific Approach to a Sharper Mind and Healthier Life. Baker Books, 2017.

25 Bernstein, Gabrielle, and Simon Schuster Audio. Judgment Detox: Release the Beliefs That Hold You Back from Living a Better Life. Simon & Schuster Audio, 2018.

26 Csikszentmihalyi, Mihaly, PhD, and Nightingale-Conant. Flow: Living at the Peak of Your Abilities. Nightingale-Conant, 2015.

27 Over the Rainbow. Harold Arlen. Leo Feist, Inc, 1939.

28 Campbell, Joseph. The Hero with A Thousand Faces. Pantheon Books, 1949.

29 Rath, T., & Clifton, D. O. (2009). How Full is your Bucket?: Positive strategies for work and life. Gallup Press.

30 Covey, Stephen. First Things First. Simon & Schuster, 1994.

31 Edwards, J. (2004). The Daffodil Principle. Shadow Mountain.

32 Kendrick, S., Kendrick, A., & Kimbrough, L. (2013). The Love Dare. B & H Publishing Group.

33 Geisel, Theodor. Yertle the Turtle and Other Stories. New York: Random House, 1950.

34 Greene, Brian. The Elegant Universe: Superstrings, Hidden Dimensions, and the Quest for the Ultimate Theory. Vintage Books, Random House, 2000.

35 Coelho, Paulo. The Alchemist. Thorsons, 1995.

36 War Room. Directed by Alex Kendrick, TriStar Pictures, 2015.

37 Wonder Woman. Directed by Patty Jenkins, Warner Bros. Pictures, 2017

38 Sneakers. Directed by Phil Alden Robinson, Universal Studios, 1992.

39 Man on Wire. Directed by James Marsh, BBC Storyville, 2008.

40 Koyaanisqatsi. Directed by Godfrey Reggio, Institute for Regional Education, 1982.

41 https://www.etymonline.com/word/talent. Accessed December 3, 2020.

42 Covey, Stephen R. The Seven Habits of Highly Effective People: Restoring the Character Ethic. New York: Simon and Schuster, 1989.

43 Keller, Gary, and Jay Papasan. The One Thing: The Surprisingly Simple Truth Behind Extraordinary Results. Austin, Tex.: Bard Press, 2012.

44 McColl, Peggy. The Won Thing: The "One" Secret to a Totally Fulfilling Life. Carlsbad, CA: Hay House, 2009.

45 Hardy, Darren. The Compound Effect. Csm, Vanguard Press, 2012.

46 Cohen, Leonard. Anthem. https://genius.com/Leonard-cohen-anthem-lyricss. Accessed August 23, 2021

47 Godfrey Saxe, John. The poems of John Godfrey Saxe. https://en.wikisource.org/wiki/The_poems_of_John_Godfrey_Saxe/The_Blind_Men_and_the_Elephant. Accessed on January 4, 2021.

48 Tozer, A. W. Whatever Happened to Worship? OM Publishing, 1985.

49 Wallace, David Foster. This Is Water: Some Thoughts, Delivered on a Significant Occasion, about Living a Compassionate Life. Little, Brown and Company, 2009.

50 Warren, Rick. The Purpose Driven Life: What on Earth Am I Here For? Grand Rapids, Mich: Zondervan, 2002.

51 Songwriters: David Allan Stewart / Glen Ballard, Ordinary Miracle lyrics © Universal Music Publishing Mgb Ltd., Universal Music Corp., Bmg Platinum Songs Us, Aerostation Corp., Arlovol Music

52 Oliver, Mary. New and Selected Poems. Beacon Press, 1992.

Made in USA - Crawfordsville, IN
96759_9781915147882
04.20.2023 1816